D1700379

RESTROOM DESIGN

daab

Society has created dozens of euphemisms to refer to the restroom and to talk about the bodily functions that occur in it, relegating it until now to the bottom of the ladder when it comes to designing public spaces. In many cases, public restrooms are associated with poor hygiene, vandalism and perversion—a place you only visit if you absolutely have to. However, smartening up in public or private places has been a feature of many civilizations throughout history, with the oldest found in the city of Mohenjo-Daro (India) from 2,000 years BC.

The evolution of the bathroom has gone hand-in-hand with the evolution of civilization, keeping abreast of changes in living conditions and different ways of understanding hygiene. This, together with the evolution in technology and the design of bathroom equipment, means the washroom is today the object of greater attention by designers, who are giving free rein to their creativity to transform it into a space of maximum comfort, with an uncommon artistic language that goes against the grain of what was the norm until now.

Today there are many public spaces in which the restroom enjoys a privileged status, making it an object of visit in bars, restaurants, airports, motorways, museums, offices, spa complexes, hospitals and hotels. Thousands of solutions are employed to merge creativity with the needs of the different groups (men, women, children, the disabled) in these spaces. Some of the examples shown here reveal this evolution with public designs for claustrophobics where the user can see everything that surrounds him outside without being seen, or bathrooms that are true artistic expressions you visit not just for physical relief but also out of aesthetic interest. In short, they are examples of the evolution of the public restroom which is today slowly approaching the collectivizing behavior it had in the past and, thanks to groundbreaking design and cutting-edge technology, is making a visit to the restroom a revelation for the senses.

Für die Verrichtung der Notdurft und den dafür vorgesehenen Ort haben sich die Menschen die unterschiedlichsten Euphemismen einfallen lassen. Öffentliche Toiletten – deren Design bis heute eine eher untergeordnete Rolle gespielt hat – werden häufig mit mangelnder Hygiene, Vandalismus und Perversion in Verbindung gebracht und lediglich im äußersten Notfall aufgesucht. Die körperliche Hygiene in öffentlichen oder privaten Räumen war jedoch im Laufe der Geschichte ein wichtiges Anliegen zahlreicher Kulturen. Die ältesten Latrinen wurden in der indischen Stadt Mohenjo-Daro gefunden und stammen aus dem 2. Jahrtausend v. Chr.

Die Entwicklung des Badezimmers verläuft parallel zu den zivilisatorischen Errungenschaften und spiegelt die sich wandelnden Lebensumstände sowie die entsprechenden Auffassungen des Begriffs Hygiene wider. Hinzu kommen der technische Fortschritt und das verbesserte Design der Badezimmerausstattung. Heute setzen Badezimmer-Designer ihre ganze kreative Kraft ein, um hochkomfortable Räume zu schaffen. Dabei bedienen sie sich einer ungewöhnlichen, als gewagt geltenden künstlerischen Sprache, die die Aufwertung des „Geheimzimmers“ in der Designwelt am besten symbolisiert.

Räume für die körperliche Hygiene stehen in einer ganzen Reihe öffentlicher Einrichtungen zur Verfügung: In Kneipen, Gaststätten, Museen, Büros, Krankenhäusern, Hotels, auf Flughäfen und Autobahnen – überall wird nach kreativen Lösungen für eine besondere Gestaltung gesucht, die mit den Bedürfnissen unterschiedlicher Personengruppen (Männer, Frauen, Kinder, Behinderte) zu vereinbaren ist. Die hier dokumentierten Entwürfe verdeutlichen die Reichweite dieser Entwicklung. So wurden für unter Platzangst leidende Personen öffentliche Toiletten entworfen, die dem Benutzer die Betrachtung der Umgebung erlauben, ohne dass er selbst gesehen wird. Der besondere künstlerische Wert anderer Projekte führt dazu, dass die sanitäre Einrichtung weniger aufgrund körperlicher Bedürfnisse als aus Interesse an der Ästhetik der Lokalität aufgesucht wird. All diese Beispiele belegen die Entwicklung, die zu den gegenwärtigen öffentlichen Toiletten geführt hat. Allmählich übernehmen sie die sozialisierende Funktion, die sie einmal besaßen, und verwandeln den Besuch des Klosetts mithilfe moderner Designkonzepte und fortschrittlichster Technologie in ein wahres Erlebnis für die Sinne.

La sociedad ha creado decenas de eufemismos para designar el baño y hablar de las funciones corporales que se realizan en él, algo que hasta ahora ha relegado este espacio a un segundo plano en la escena del diseño. En muchos casos, los servicios públicos se asocian con sitios poco higiénicos, objeto de vandalismo y perversiones, a los que sólo se acude en casos de extrema necesidad. Sin embargo, el aseo del cuerpo en lugares públicos o privados ha estado presente en muchas de las civilizaciones a lo largo de la historia. Los baños más antiguos se sitúan en la ciudad de Mohenjo-Daro (India) y datan de 2.000 años a. C.

La evolución del baño ha ido paralela a la de la civilización, de acuerdo con las mutaciones de las condiciones de vida y las diferentes formas de entender la higiene. Todo esto, sumado al desarrollo de la tecnología y el diseño de equipamientos, ha logrado que actualmente el sanitario reciba más atención por parte de los diseñadores, quienes dan rienda suelta a su creatividad para crear espacios cómodos y con un lenguaje artístico inusual, contrario a lo establecido hasta ahora.

Hoy en día son numerosos los lugares públicos en los que el aseo goza de un estatus privilegiado y es objeto de visita: bares, restaurantes, aeropuertos, autopistas, museos, oficinas, *spas*, hospitales, hoteles; son miles las soluciones empleadas para fusionar la creatividad con las necesidades de los diferentes colectivos (hombres, mujeres, niños, inválidos). Algunos ejemplos que se muestran a continuación ponen de manifiesto los diversos cambios en los proyectos públicos: sanitarios para claustrofóbicos, donde el usuario –sin ser visto– puede ver todo lo que lo rodea; o baños que se convierten en auténticas expresiones artísticas, que llevan al usuario a entrar en ellos no sólo por el desahogo físico, sino también por el interés estético. En definitiva, ejemplos todos de la evolución del baño público, que se acerca poco a poco a las conductas socializantes que tuvo en otros tiempos y que consigue, de la mano del diseño más vanguardista y de la tecnología más puntera, que la visita al excusado sea una revelación para los sentidos.

La société a créé des dizaines d'euphémismes pour désigner les toilettes et parler des fonctions corporelles qui s'y déroulent, en le reléguant jusqu'à maintenant au second plan en matière de design d'espaces publics. Bien souvent, les toilettes publiques évoquent des endroits peu hygiéniques, objets de vandalisme et de perversions, auxquels on ne se rend qu'en cas de nécessité absolue. Néanmoins, la toilette du corps dans des lieux publics ou privés a été présente dans de nombreuses civilisations au fil de l'histoire, les exemples les plus anciens ayant été retrouvés dans la ville de Mohenjo-Daro (Inde), 2 000 ans av. J.-C.

L'évolution des toilettes s'est faite en parallèle de celle de la civilisation, en fonction des mutations des conditions de vie et des diverses interprétations de l'hygiène. Assortie d'avancées technologiques et de la fabrication d'équipements correspondants, cette évolution a permis que les sanitaires soient à présent davantage pris en considération par les designers. Ces derniers laissent ainsi aller leur créativité pour les transformer en espaces de confort maximal, avec un langage artistique peu habituel qui combat ce qui était établi jusqu'alors.

À l'heure actuelle, bon nombre d'espaces publics (bars, restaurants, aéroports, autoroutes, musées, bureaux, spas, hôpitaux, hôtels) accordent une place privilégiée aux toilettes, qui deviennent des lieux de visite. Une foule de solutions sont appliquées pour fusionner créativité et besoins des différents groupes de population (hommes, femmes, enfants, handicapés) dans ces espaces. Certains exemples dans les pages qui suivent soulignent cette évolution avec des projets publics pour personnes claustrophobes, dans lesquels l'usager peut voir tout ce qui l'entoure à l'extérieur sans être vu, ou encore des toilettes qui deviennent de véritables expressions artistiques auxquelles l'usager se rend non seulement pour ses besoins physiques, mais aussi pour leur intérêt esthétique. En fin de compte, autant d'exemples de l'évolution des toilettes publiques actuelles qui se rapprochent peu à peu des conduites socialisantes d'époques antérieures, en faisant que le design plus avant-gardiste et la technologie de pointe transforment la visite au petit coin en une révélation pour tous les sens.

La società ha creato decine di eufemismi per indicare il bagno e per parlare delle funzioni corporali che vi si compiono, un ambiente che fino ad ora è rimasto confinato su un piano secondario sulla scena del design degli spazi pubblici. In molti casi, i servizi pubblici sono associati a luoghi poco igienici, oggetto di vandalismo e perversioni, nei quali si entra solo in caso di estrema necessità. Tuttavia, l'igiene del corpo in luoghi pubblici o privati, è stata presente in molte delle civiltà nel corso della storia; gli esempi più antichi si trovano nella città di Mohenjo-Daro (India), 2.000 anni prima di Cristo.

L'evoluzione del bagno è stata parallela a quella della civiltà, ed è avvenuta in base alle mutazioni delle condizioni di vita e delle diverse forme d'intendere l'igiene. Tutto questo, sommato all'evoluzione della tecnologia e del design di installazioni per il bagno, è riuscito a fare in modo che i sanitari siano, nell'attualità, maggiormente considerati da parte dei designer, che applicano la loro creatività per convertirli in spazi di massimo confort, con un linguaggio artistico poco usuale che si ribella contro quanto stabilito fino ad ora.

Sono attualmente numerosi gli spazi pubblici in cui l'igiene gode di uno status privilegiato, convertendosi in un luogo da visitare: bar, ristoranti, aeroporti, autostrade, musei, uffici, *stabilimenti termali*, ospedali, alberghi; sono migliaia le soluzioni adottate per fondere la creatività con le necessità dei vari collettivi (uomini, donne, bambini, invalidi) in questi spazi. Alcuni esempi riportati qui sotto mettono in luce questa evoluzione con progetti pubblici per persone affette da claustrofobia, in cui l'utente può vedere tutto ciò che lo circonda all'esterno senza essere visto, o bagni che diventano vere e proprie espressioni artistiche che l'utenza visita non solo per un bisogno fisiologico, ma anche per l'interesse estetico. Si tratta, in definitiva, di esempi dell'evoluzione del bagno pubblico attuale, che si avvicina a poco a poco ai comportamenti socializzanti che si verificarono in altre epoche, facendo in modo, con l'aiuto del design più all'avanguardia e della tecnologia più innovativa, che la visita alla latrina sia una rivelazione per i sensi.

123DV ARCHITECTUUR & CONSULT | ROTTERDAM
RESTROOMS IN JAARBEURS UTRECHT
Utrecht, The Netherlands | 2007

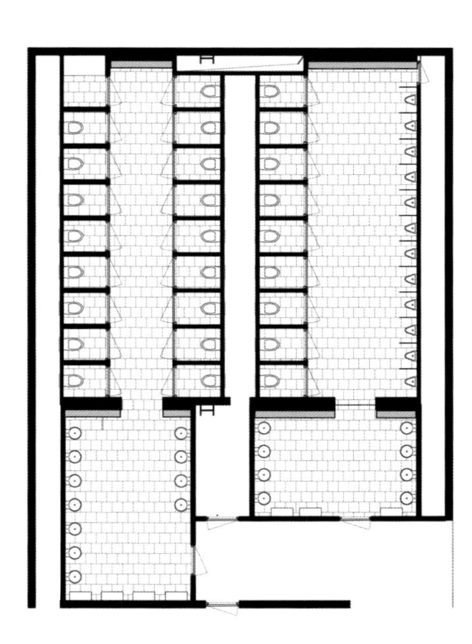

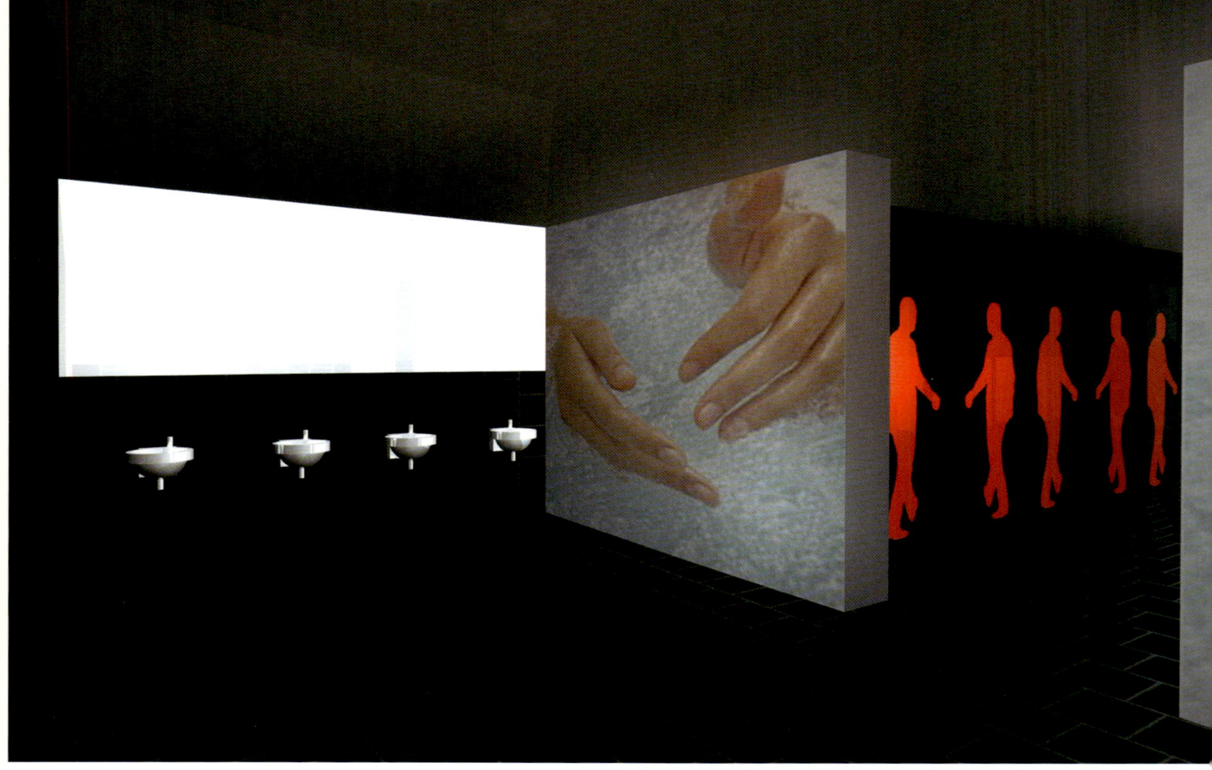

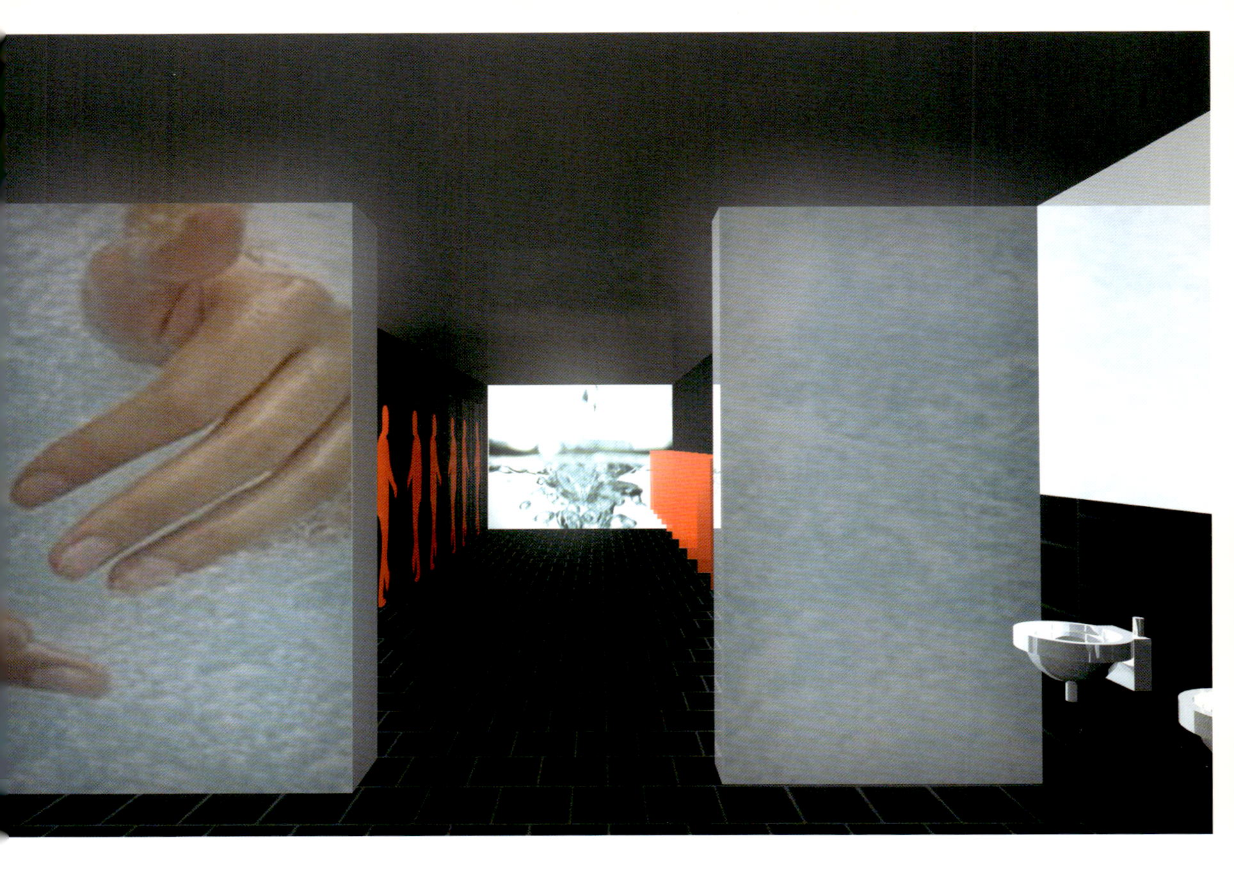

3DELUXE | WIESBADEN

COCOON CLUB

Frankfurt, Germany | 2004

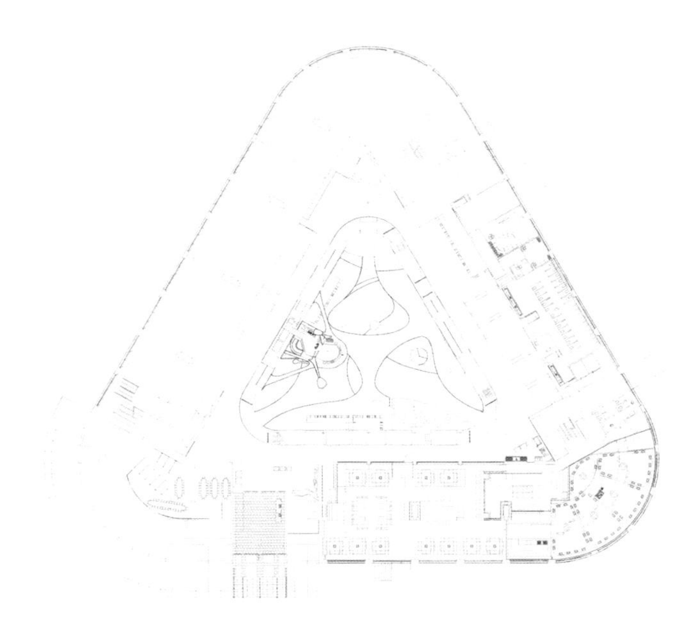

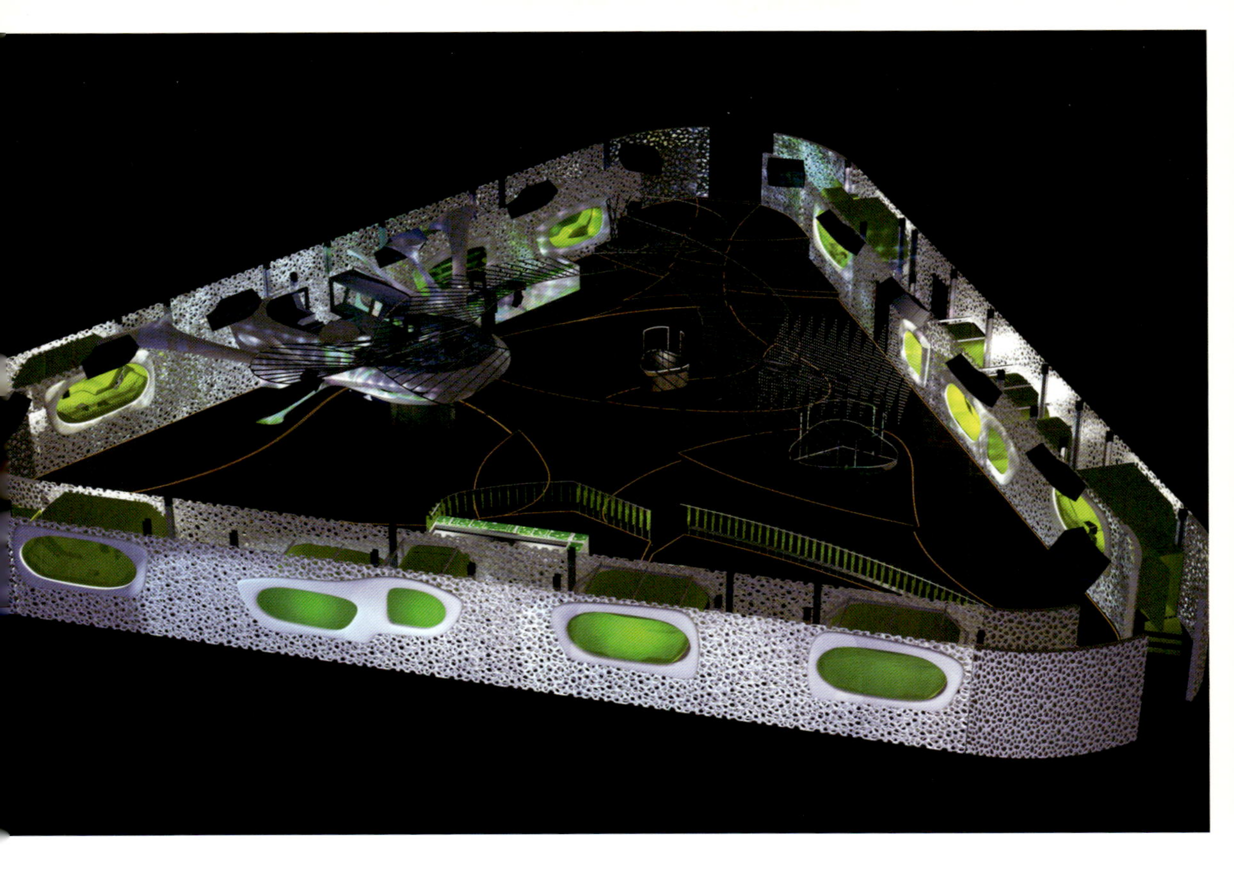

3RW ARCHITECTS, SMEDSVIG LANDSKAPSARKITEKTER | BERGEN

FLYDALSJUVET VIEWPOINT AND SERVICE BUILDINGS

Geiranger, Norway | 2006

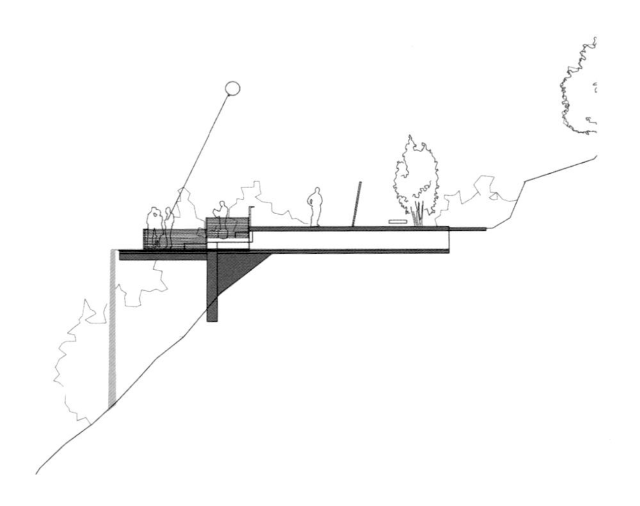

3RW ARCHITECTS | BERGEN
HEREIANE SERVICE BUILDING
Hardanger, Norway | 2007

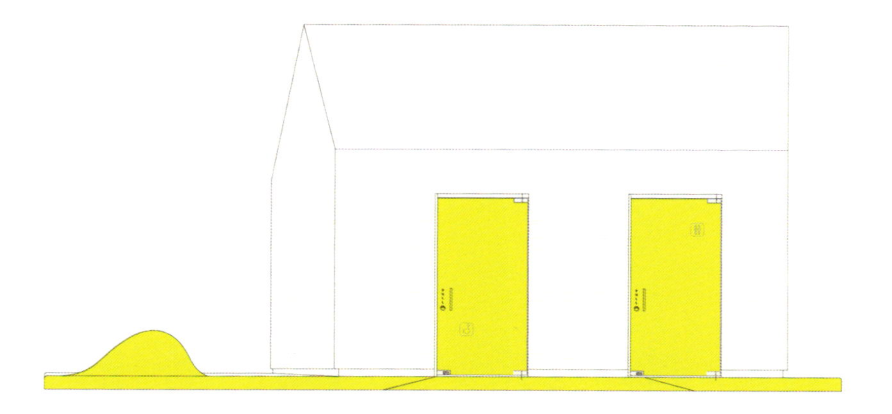

ACCONCI STUDIO | NEW YORK
PURPUR. ARCHITEKTUR | VIENNA
MURINSEL
Graz, Austria | 2003

ALONSO BALAGUER & ARQUITECTOS ASOCIADOS | BARCELONA
DUET SPORTS
Tiana, Barcelona, Spain | 2005

ALONSO BALAGUER & ARQUITECTOS ASOCIADOS | BARCELONA
O2 FITNESS CENTER
Barcelona, Spain | 2005

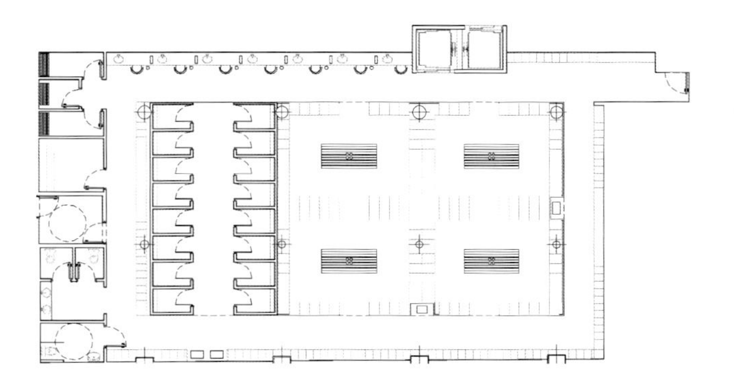

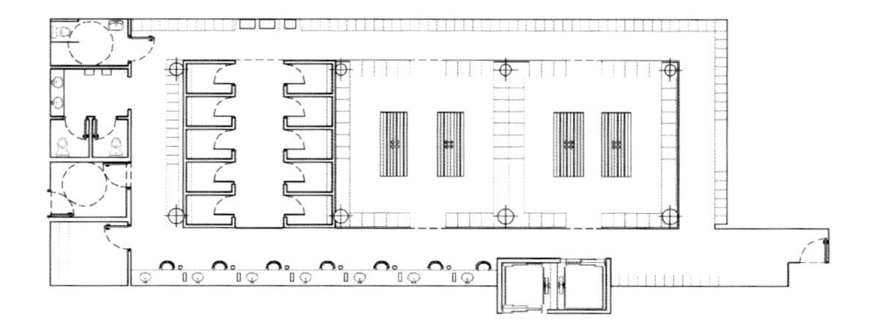

duchas

AMALGAM | LONDON

BULLRING SHOPPING CENTER

Birmingham, United Kingdom | 2003

ULLRING

SALA
5
20:00
19:50
5

ANDREA VIVIANI | PADOVA

MULTIPLEX CINECITY TRIESTE

Pradamano, Udine, Italy | 2002

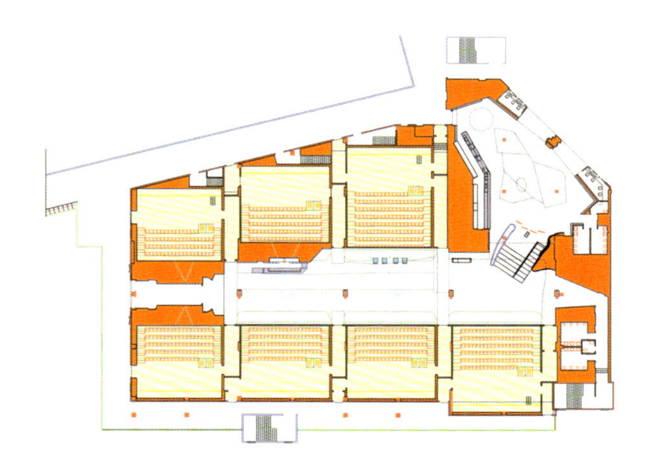

TOILETTE

UOMO

ARCHITECTURE WORKSHOP | WELLINGTON

ORIENTAL PARADE

Wellington, New Zealand | 2005

AIRTRONIC

ATELIER VAN LIESHOUT | ROTTERDAM

TOILET UNITS MUSEUM BOIJMANS VAN BEUNINGEN

Rotterdam, The Netherlands | 1998

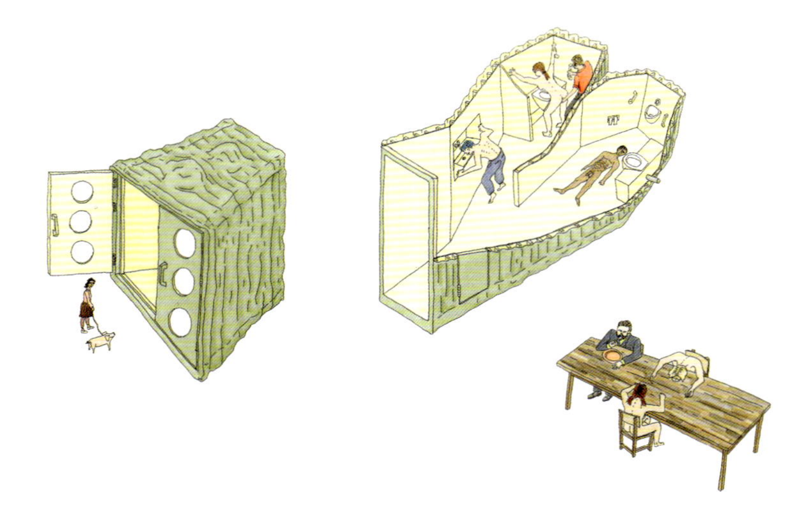

DAMES

BLOBB/ANALÍA SEGAL | BROOKLYN
BLOBB
Brooklyn, NY, USA | 2006

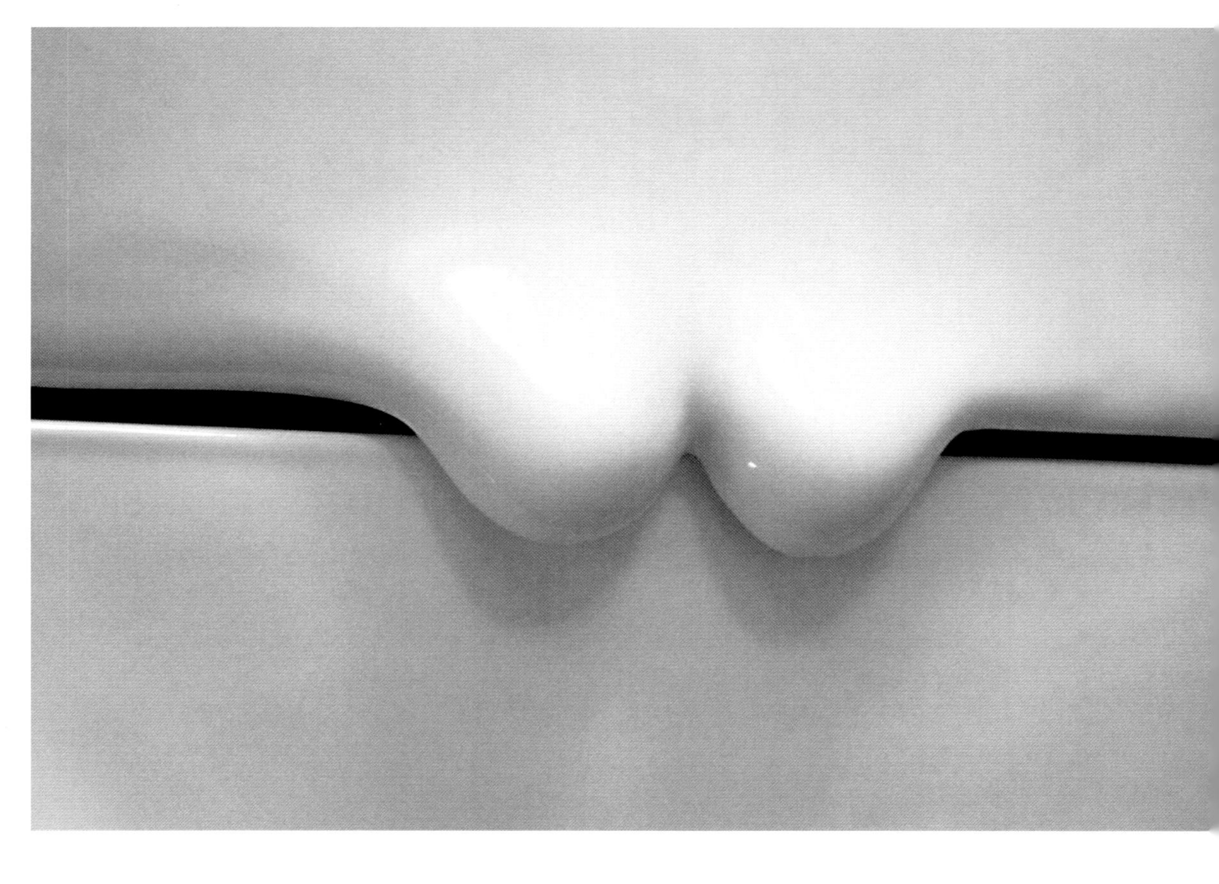

BOB COPRAY, ANTHONY KLEINEPIER | EINDHOVEN

DE EFFENAAR

Eindhoven, The Netherlands | 2005

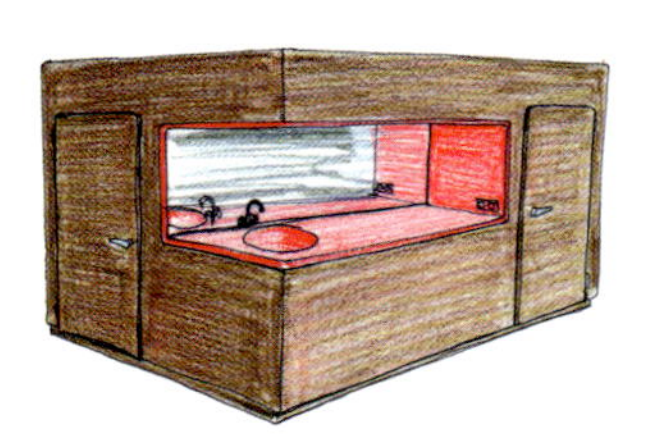

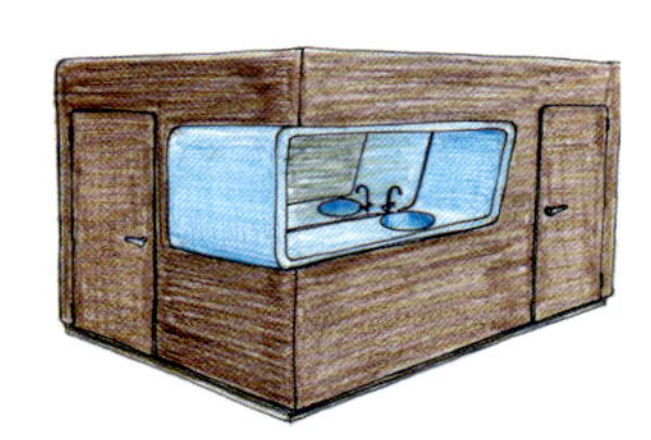

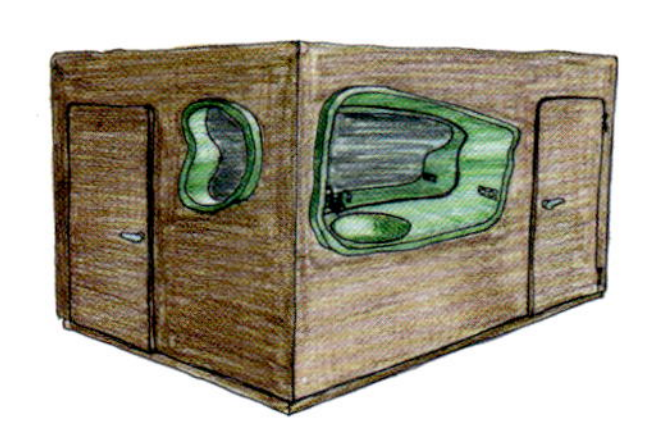

Jo Shmo's

BUCKLEY GRAY YEOMAN | LONDON

JO SHMO

Wimbledon, London, United Kingdom | 2003

Girls
Boys
Girls
Boys
Girls
Boys

Girls

Boys

CAMENZIND EVOLUTION | ZÜRICH

SIEMENS RESTAURANTS

Zurich, Switzerland | 2002

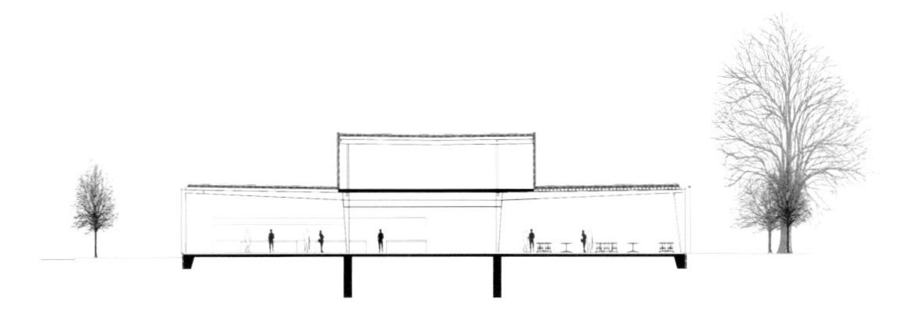

CHANGDUK KIM & YOUNGKI HONG | SEOUL

UNIVERSAL TOILET

Seoul, South Korea | 2007

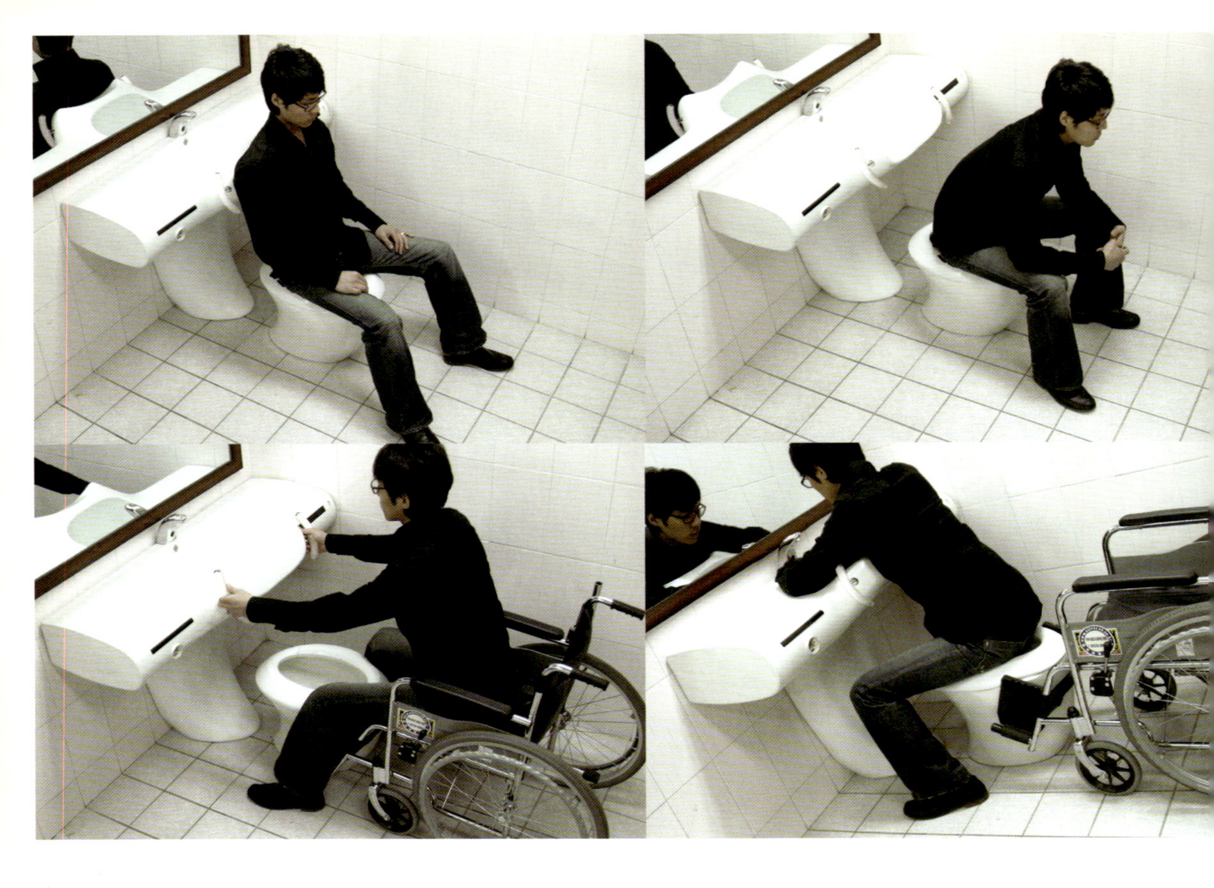

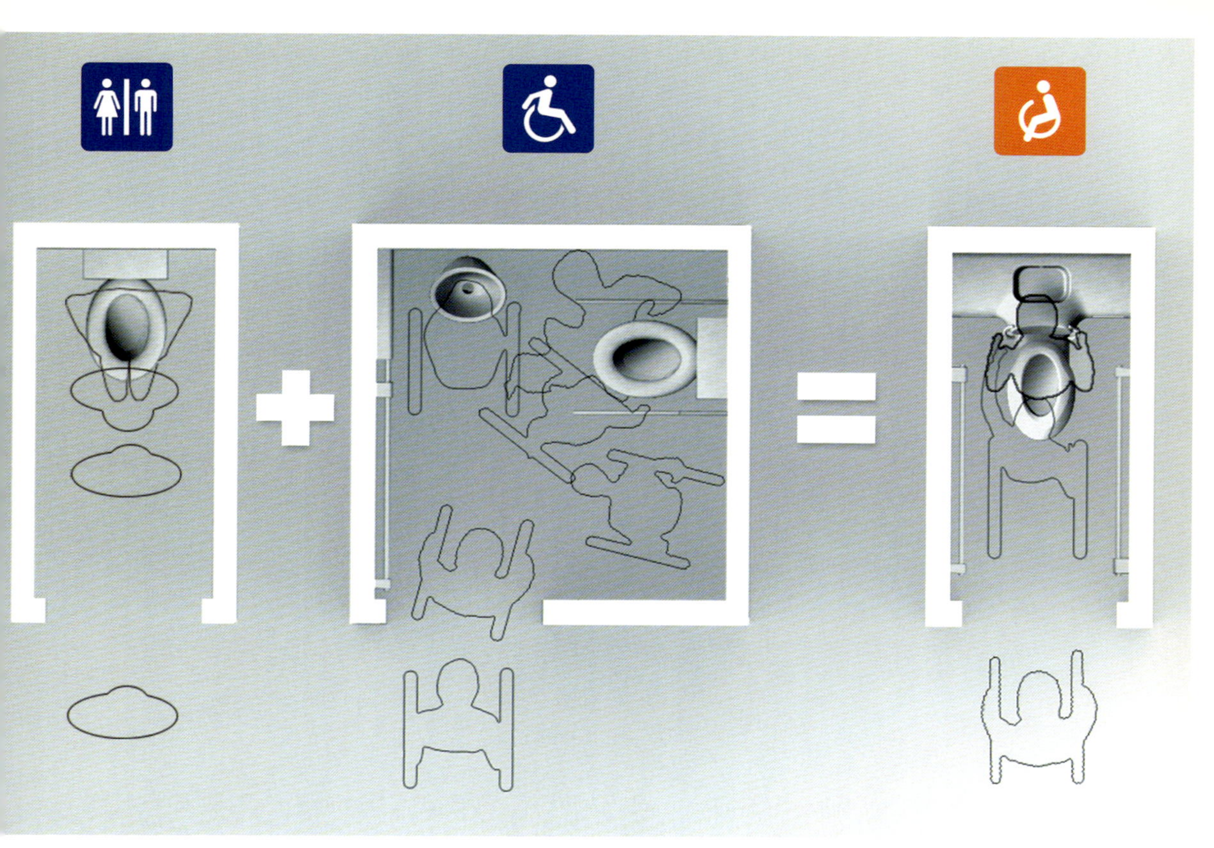

DAVID COLLINS STUDIO | LONDON
KABARETS PROPHECY
London, United Kingdom | 2004

QUEEN OF THE
TEXAS
HOLD-EM.
KNOWN FROM MONTE
CARLO TO THE STRIP
THIS LADY'S GOT MORE
HUSTLE THAN LARRY
FLYNT. OMAHA'S
DOMINANT HAND
SHUFFLES THE DECK
WITH SO MUCH DASH
AND PANACHE THAT
YOU'LL BLOW YOUR
WAD ON THE FLOP
BUT YOU CAN BET
YOUR BOTTOM
DOLLAR THAT
SHE'S FAKING
IT LEAVING
YOU TO MUCK
YOUR OWN HAND.
WHETHER IT'S ALL IN
BACKDOOR NUT
OMAHA

SACKFUL SMYTHE
THE KABARET PROFIT OF PROFIT WITH
THE BABY-BLING. PRAYER BEADS AND
RING THAT HOLDS THE KEY TO
DESTINY'S DOOR. YOUR NAME ON THE
LIST? UNDERDRESSED. CRASS AND
PISSED? WRONG HAIR. WRONG DAY.
WRONG PROFESSION? TO ENTER
SHANGRILA. THEN PASS MUSTER
PAST BOY WONDER YOU MUST.
BUT YOU MUST HAVE BECAUSE
YOU'RE HERE...
...SO BELIEVE.

AIR KISSING. BOTH WAY BENDING. TEENAGE SHOWER NOZZLE DREAM BOAT.
ACTING WITH NO HOPE. EULOGISING ON CURRENT WORLD AFFAIRS.
HYDROPONIC DOPE. ALL CHARISMA KNOWING HUMOUR AND SLY BAD-BOY CHARM IN
FLIP-FLOPS. BARE CHEST AND FUR COAT ON LOW CARB, NO CARB. VODKA AND
SODA MIXED UP WITH BIKRAM YOGA.

DICK
STYLE STUD AND HE-HUNK HUNG
LIKE A SARTORIAL
CLOTHESHORSE
WARD

DESIGNRICHTUNG | ZURICH
GEBERIT HEADQUARTERS
Jona, Switzerland | 2003

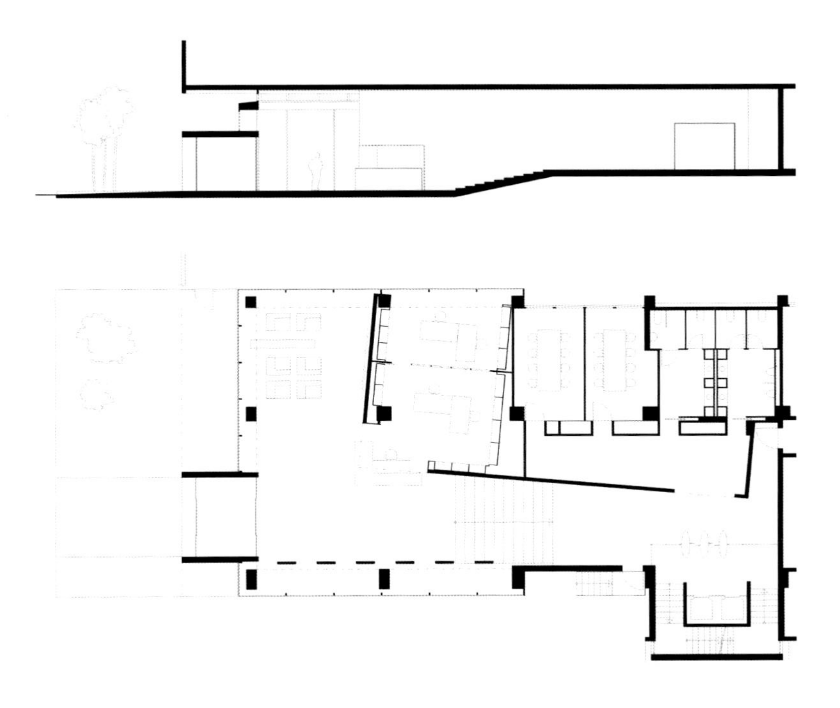

Empfang 2

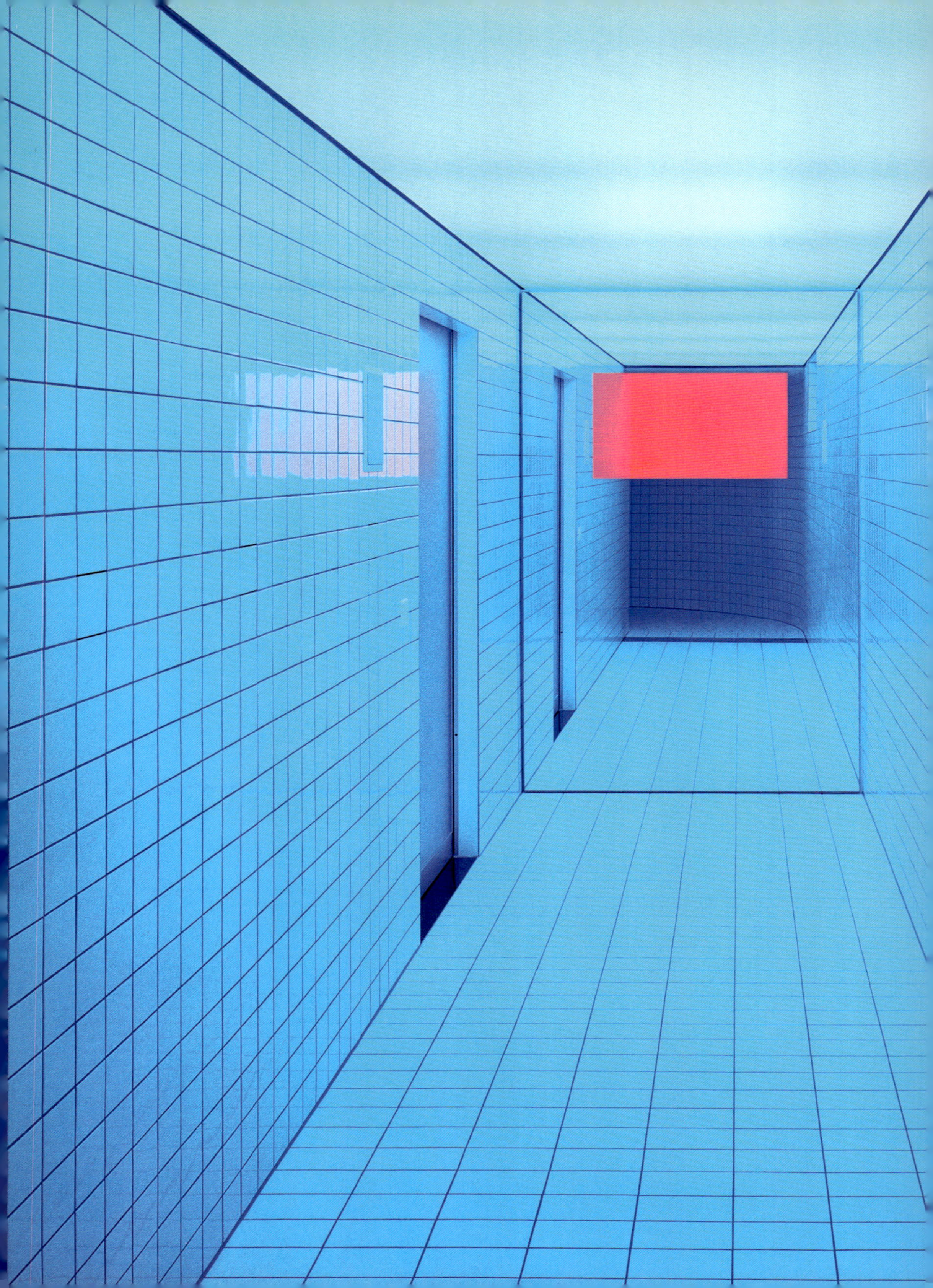

DESIGNRICHTUNG | ZURICH
GEBERIT TRAINING CENTER
Jona, Switzerland | 2003

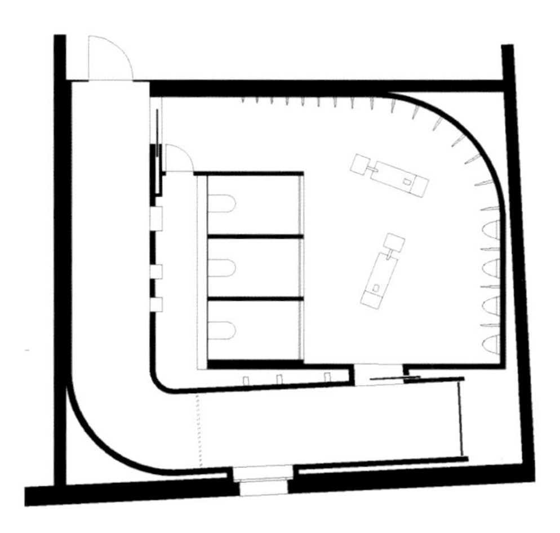

1

DIZEL & SATE | STOCKHOLM
ASTORIA
Stockholm, Sweden | 2004

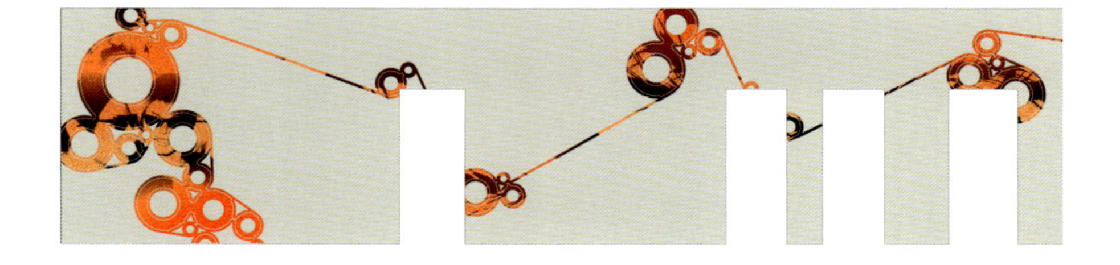

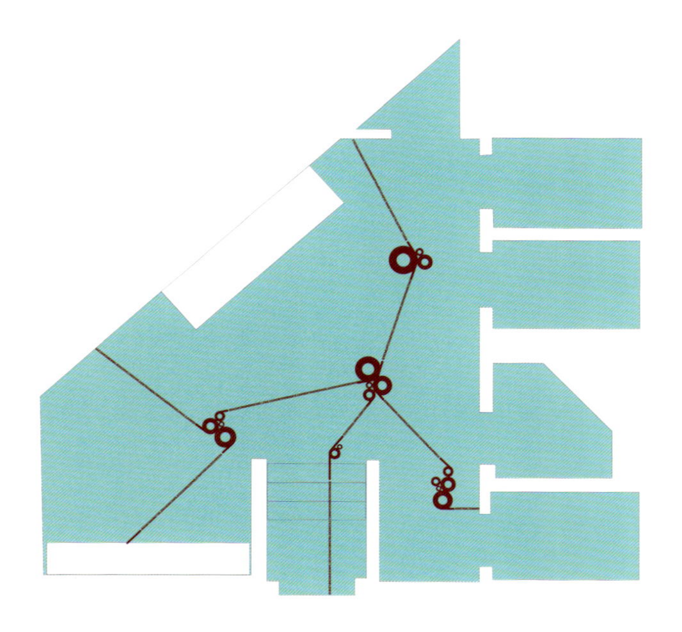

GAELGARCÍABERNALBENICIODELTOROCARLOSREYGADASALFONSOCUARÓNDIE
IÑÁRRITUDANNYTREJODAMIAN

Dalai

ELIA FELICES | BARCELONA

DALAI DISCOTHEQUE

Sabadell, Spain | 2006

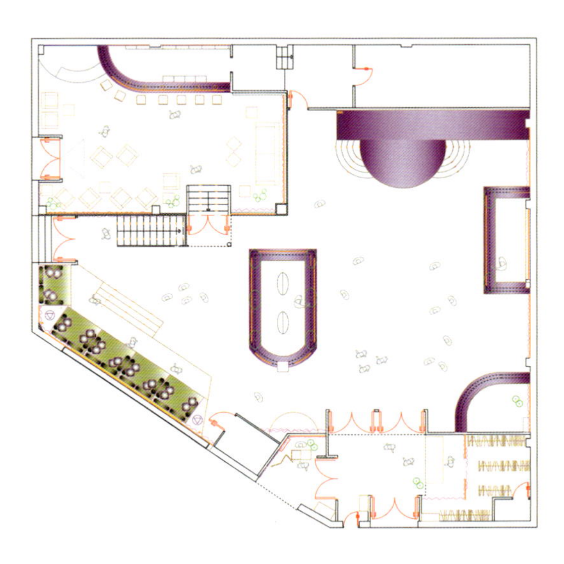

GARCÍA & RUIZ ARCHITECTURE DESIGN | MADRID

CEPSA RESTROOMS

Madrid, Spain | 2007

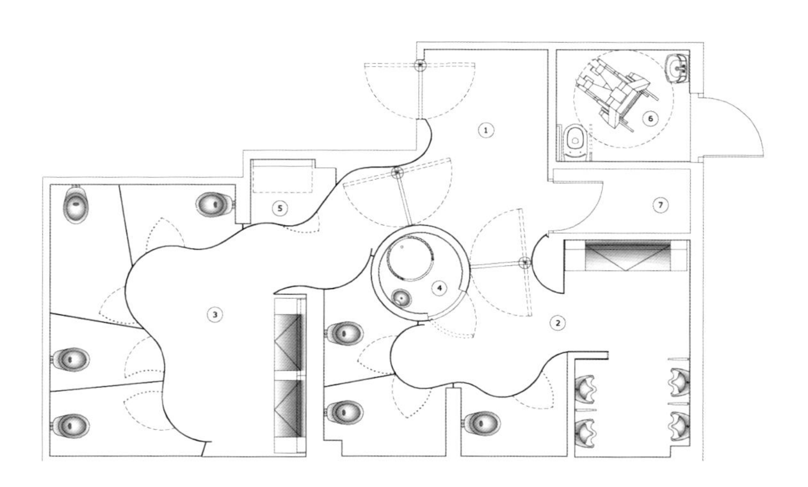

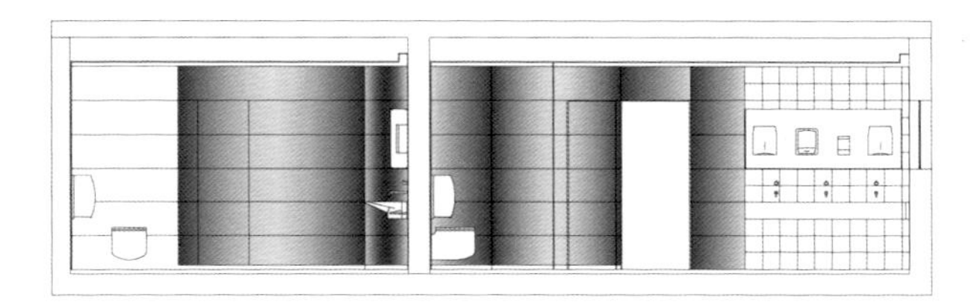

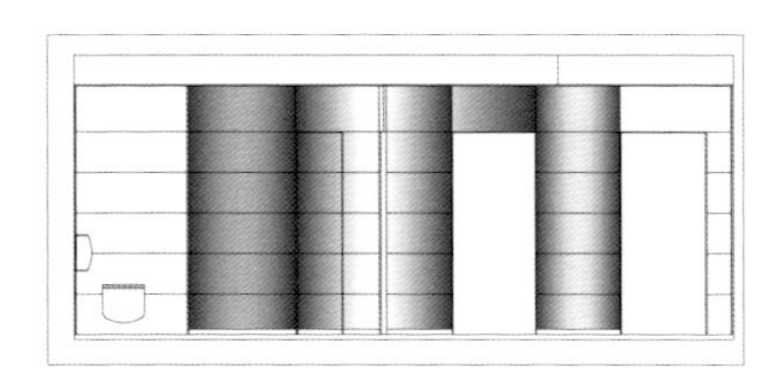

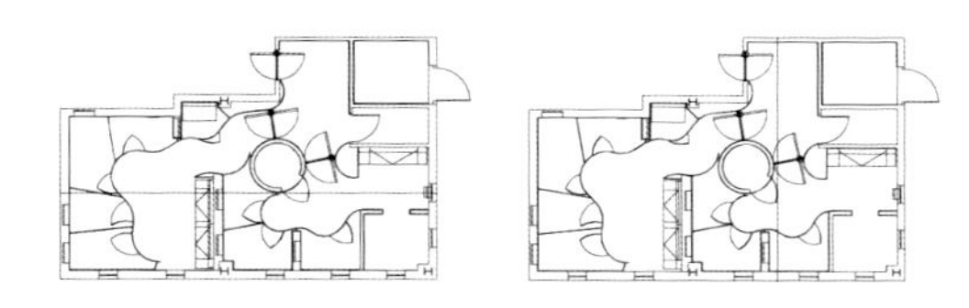

GERMÁN DEL SOL | SANTIAGO DE CHILE
BATHS IN ATACAMA
San Pedro de Atacama, Chile | 2005

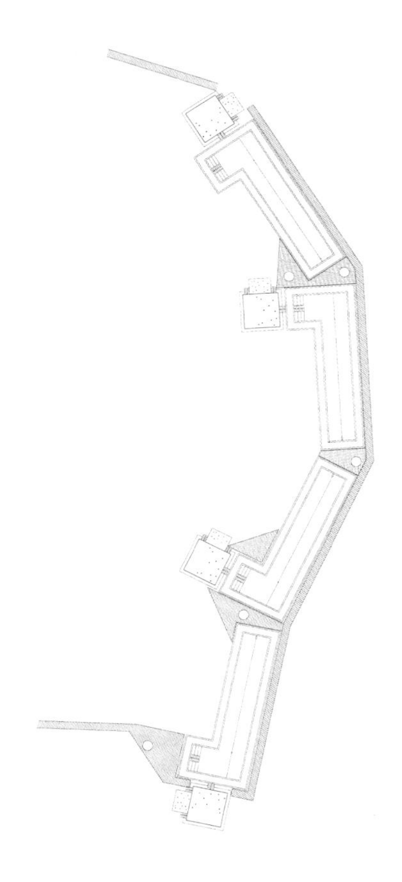

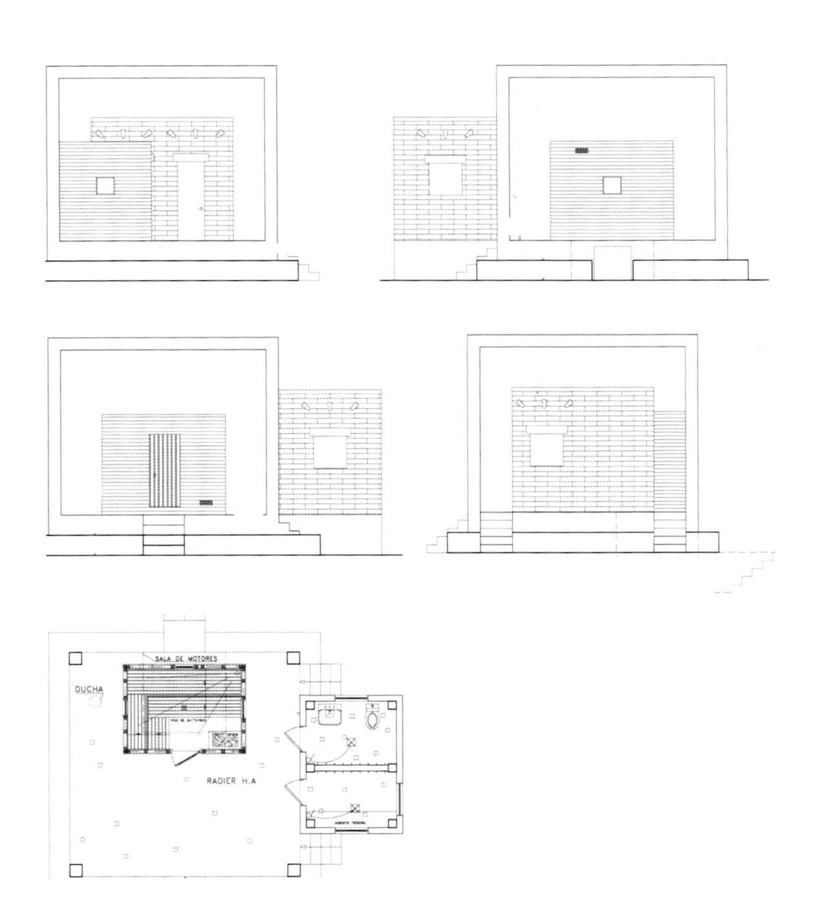
SALA DE MOTORES
DUCHA
RADIER H.A

NO ENTRY
WRONG WAY

GREGORY BURGESS ARCHITECTS | VICTORIA

HIGHWAY REST AREAS

Ravenswood, and Mangalore, Australia | 2005

M

M

HASSAN ABDULLAH | LONDON
LES TROIS GARÇONS
London, United Kingdom | 2005

HŠH ARCHITECTS | OLOMOUC
ARCHDIOCESAN MUSEUM IN OLOMOUC
Olomouc, Czech Republic | 2006

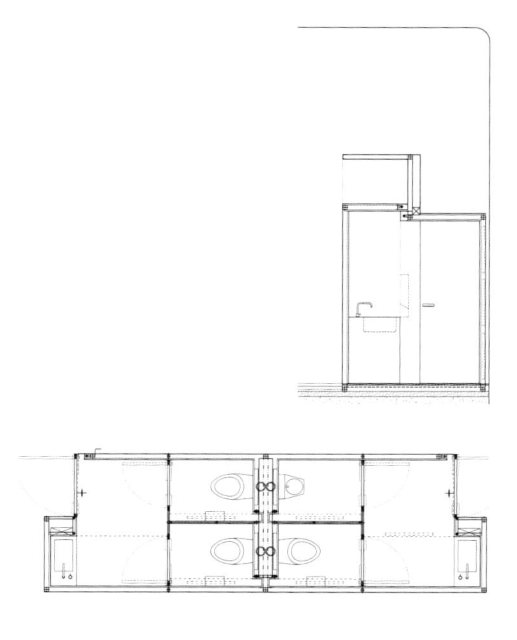

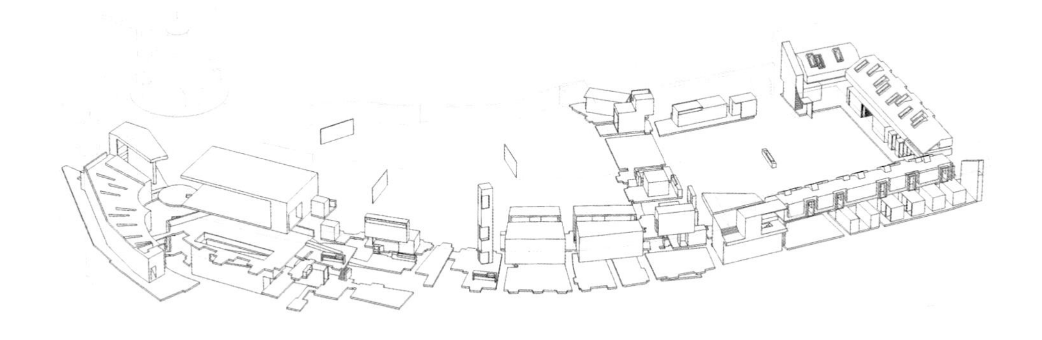

JESTICO & WHILES | LONDON

PRINCESS DIANA OF WALES MEMORIAL PLAYGROUND

London, United Kingdom | 2002

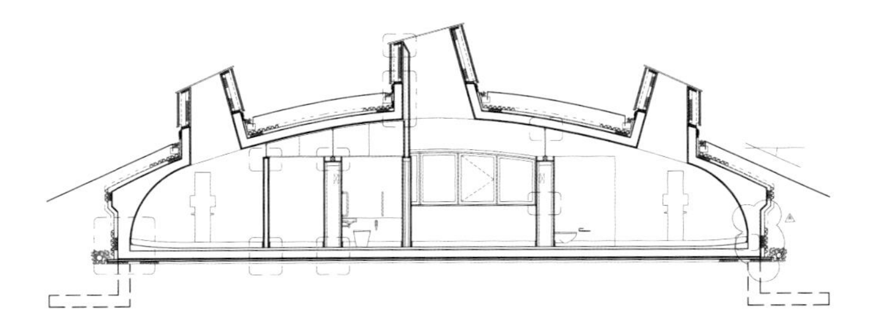

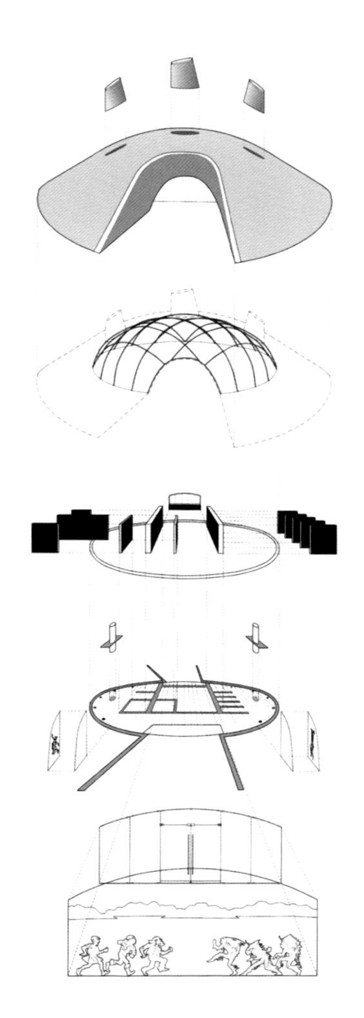

JESTICO & WHILES | LONDON
VILLAGE CINEMAS MULTIPLEX
Praga, Czeck Republic | 2003

JOHANNES TORPE | COPENHAGEN
NASA
Copenhagen, Denmark | 2002

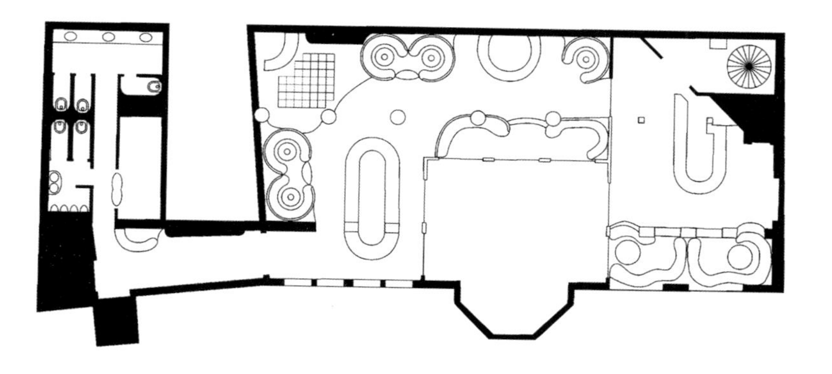

KADAWITTFELDARCHITEKTUR | AACHEN
ZEUGHAUS
Aachen, Austria | 2006

KRASKE ARCHITECTURE & YACHT DESIGN | MUNICH
TANTRIS
Munich, Germany | 2008

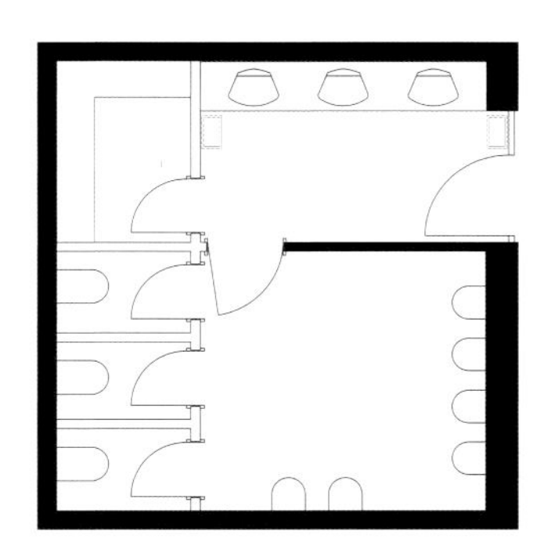

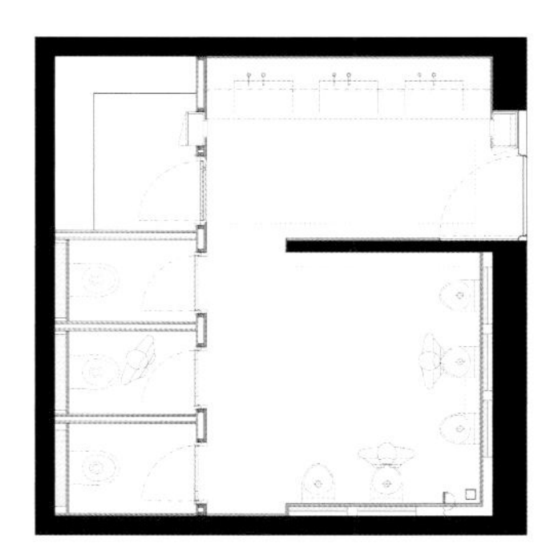

Serviced Offices-IT and Telecoms

LACOCK GULLAM | LONDON
BUTTERFLY ON-STREET URINAL
London, United Kingdom | 2002

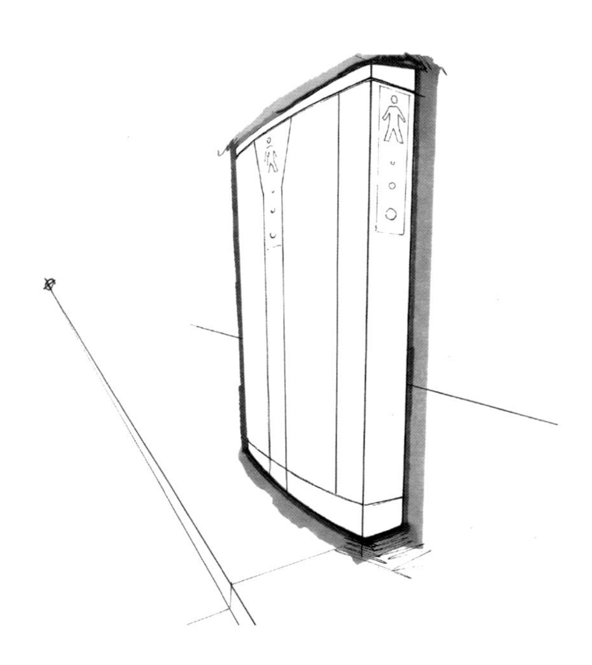

Urinal
When Closed Use 24 Hour Accessible Toilet in - Broadwick Street
For Details of Other Toilets and Times of Opening Telephone 020 7641 2000
No Motor Vehicles

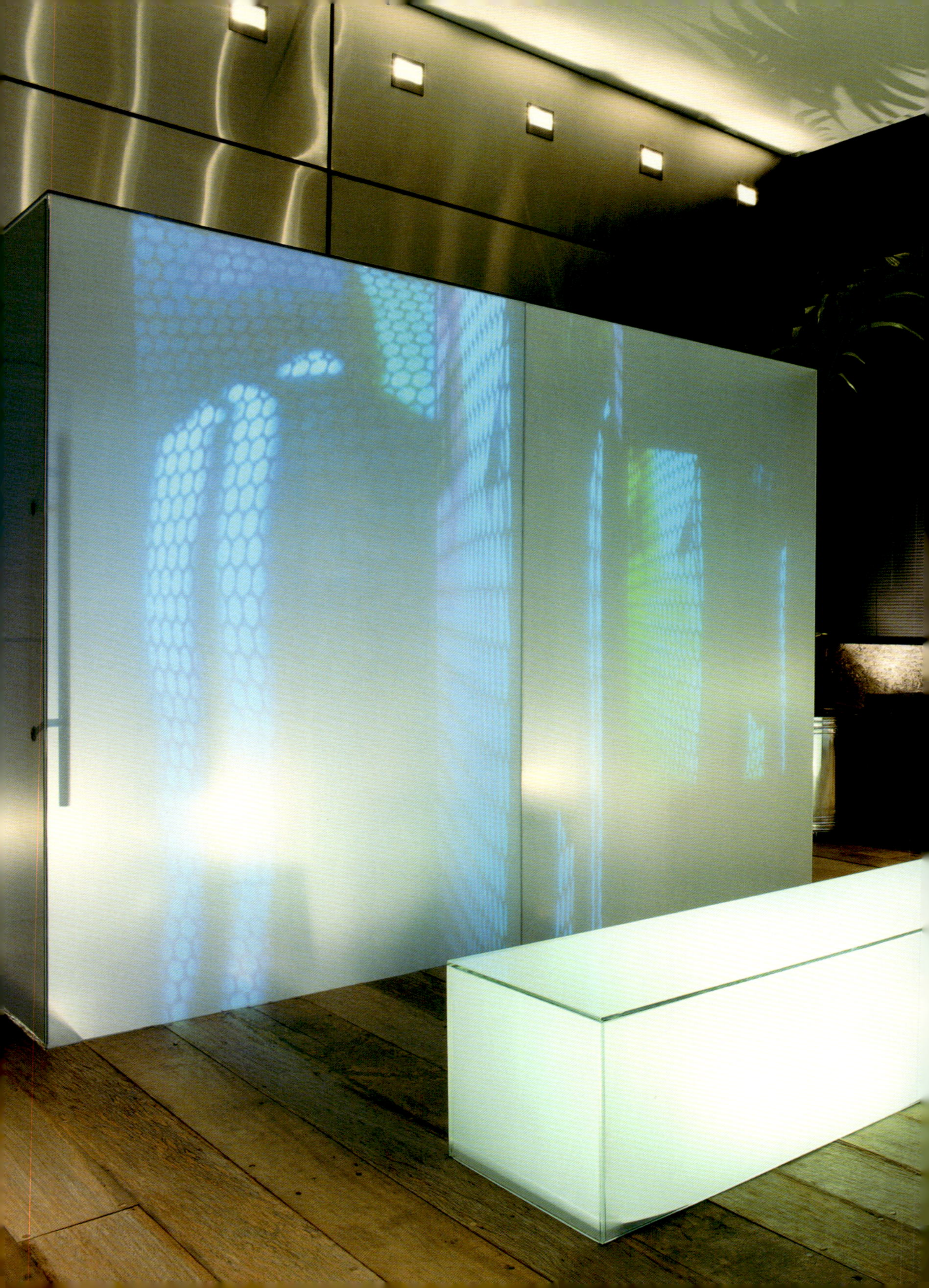

MARCELO SODRÉ | SÃO PAULO

CASACOR

São Paulo, Brazil | 2003

WC

MATALI CRASSET PRODUCTIONS | PARIS
HI HOTEL
Nice, France | 2004

MIRÓ RIVERA ARCHITECTS | AUSTIN

LADY BIRD LAKE HIKE AND BIKE TRAIL RESTROOM

Austin, TX, USA | 2008

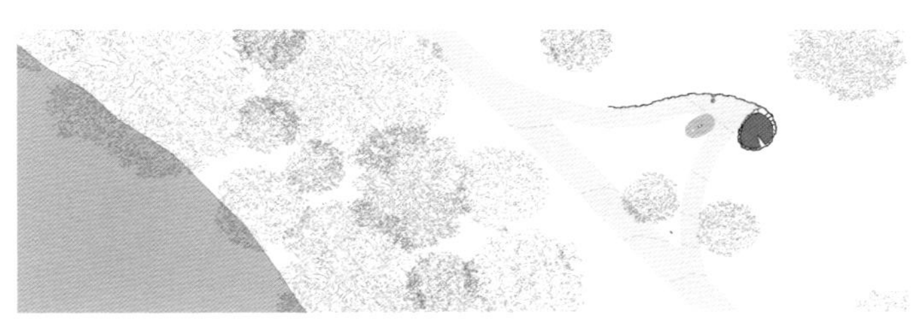

WOMEN
MEN

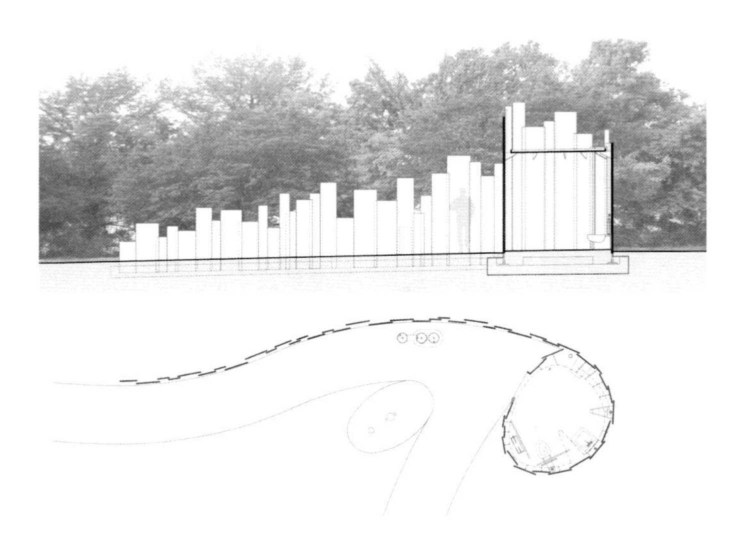

WOMEN
MEN

POSSIBLE BY:
LAKE TRAIL FOUNDATION
ARCHITECTS
FOUNDATION
CREATION DEPARTMENT
ENGINEERING
SURVEY COMPANY, INC.
2007

OBECO

MONICA BONVICINI | MILAN

DON'T MISS A SEC

Basel, Switzerland/Rotterdam, The Netherlands | 2004

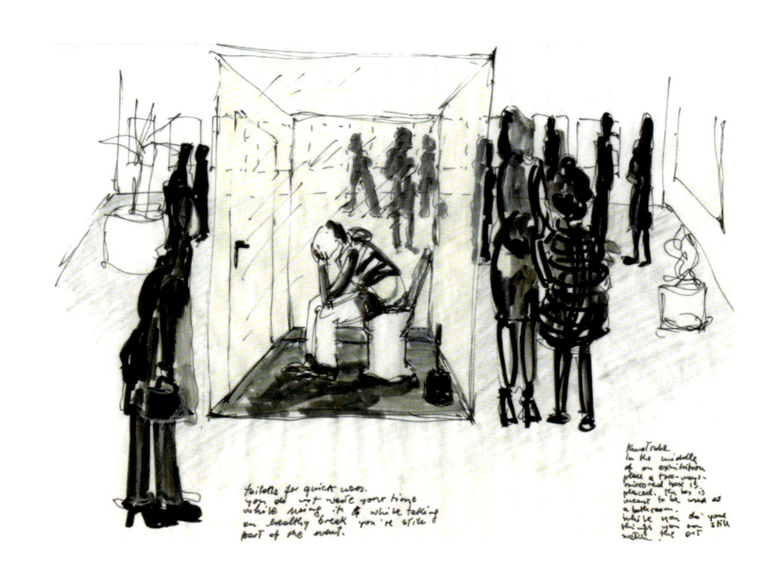

in the middle of
attention quick
no time to loose
enjoy art while
Art & needs
KUNST RUHE

LLOYD:HOTEL

MVRDV | ROTTERDAM
LLOYD HOTEL
Amsterdam, The Netherlands | 2004

PENTAGRAM | NEW YORK

LOCKER ROOMS AND BATHROOMS IN ARIZONA CARDINALS STADIUM

Phoenix, AZ, USA | 2007

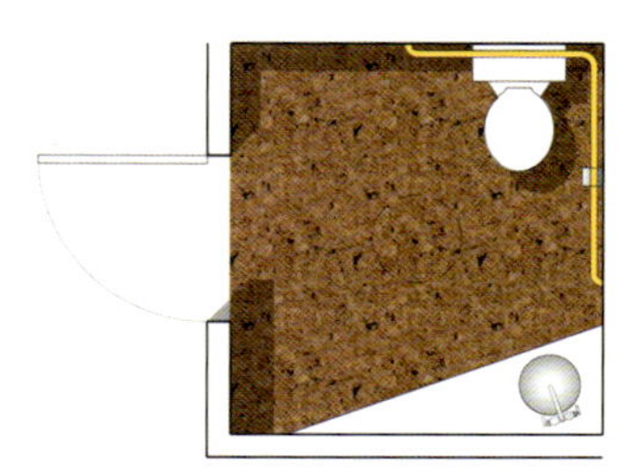

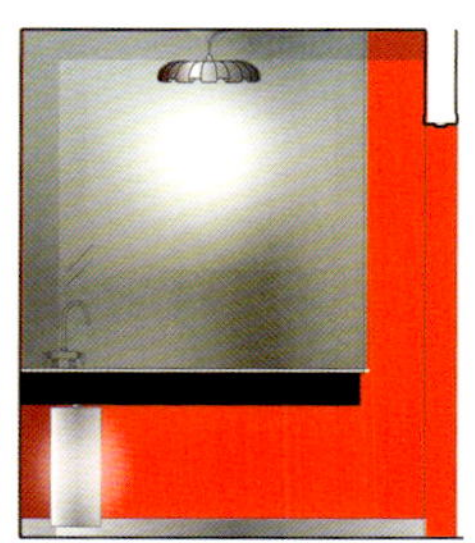

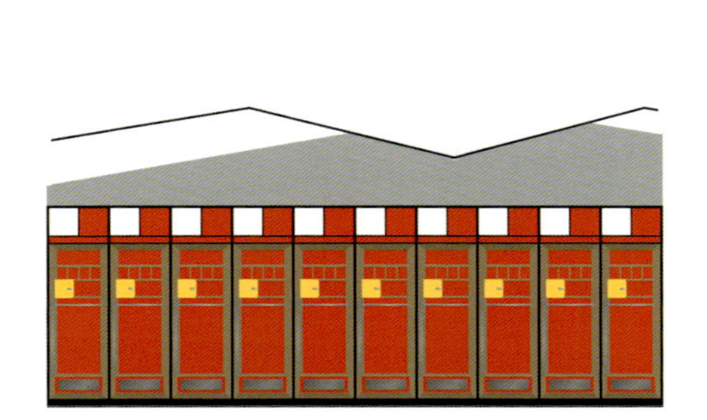

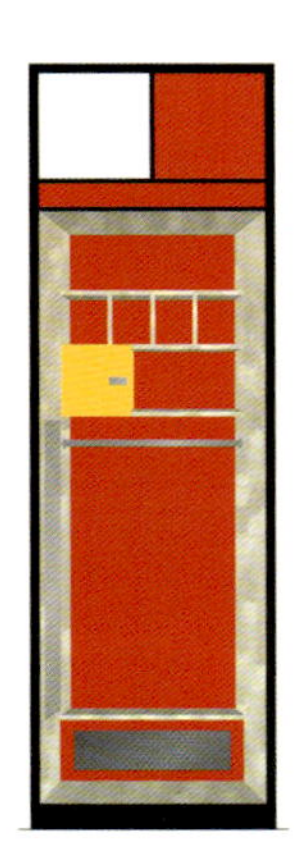

PIERLUIGI PIU | CAGLIARI

OLIVOMARE RESTAURANT

London, United Kingdom | 2007

PLASTIK ARCHITECTS | LONDON
GRAVESEND PUBLIC TOILETS
Gravesend, United Kingdom | 2006

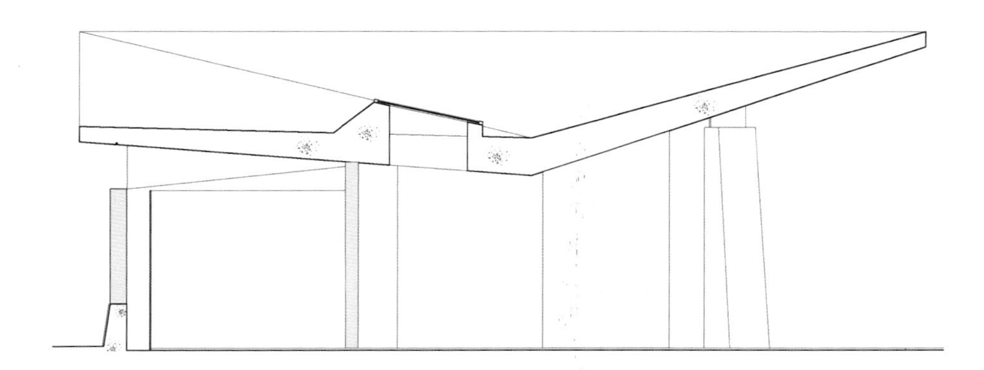

LETS

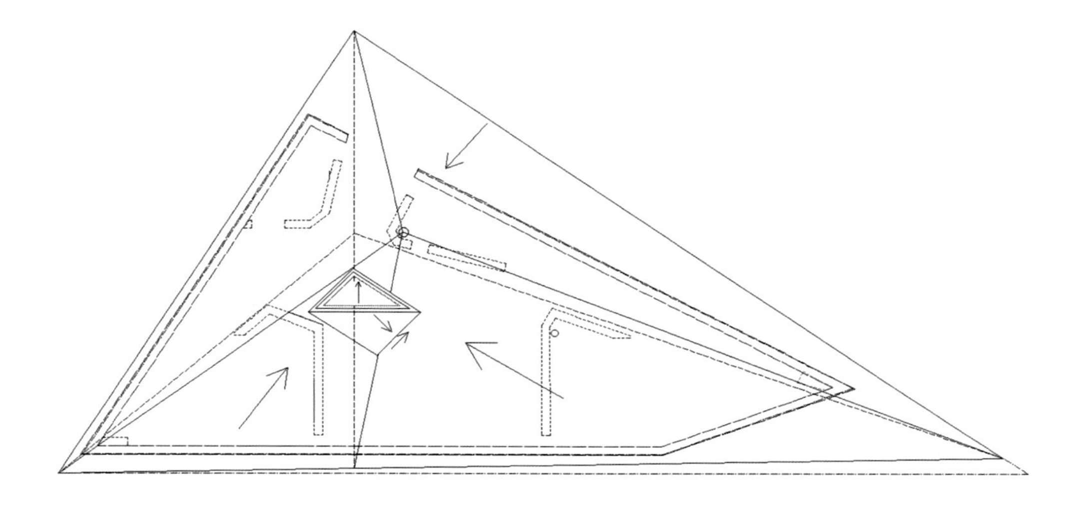

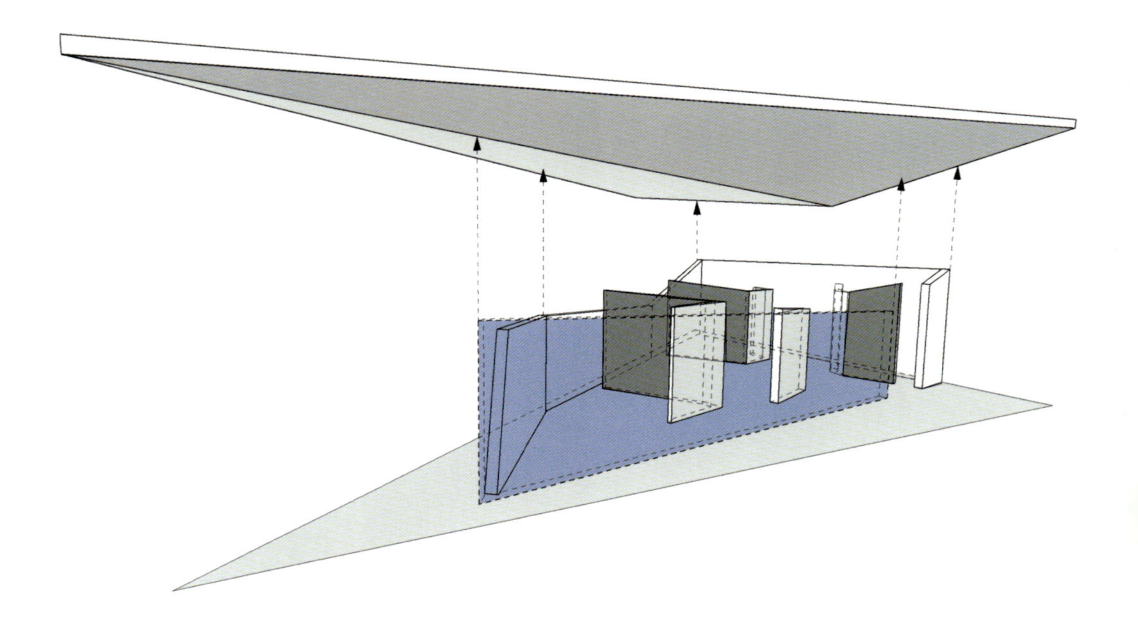

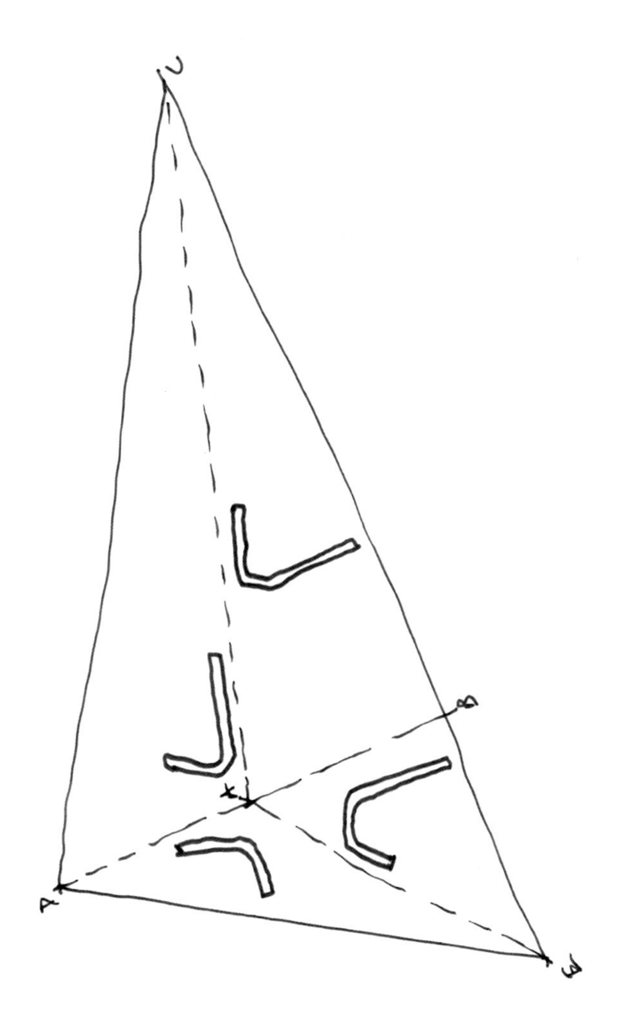

PLAYGROUND MELBOURNE/FADY HACHEM | MELBOURNE

VALVE

Melbourne, Australia | 2007

RCR ARANDA PIGEM VILALTA ARQUITECTES | OLOT
PAVILIONS IN LES COLS RESTAURANT
Olot, Spain | 2006

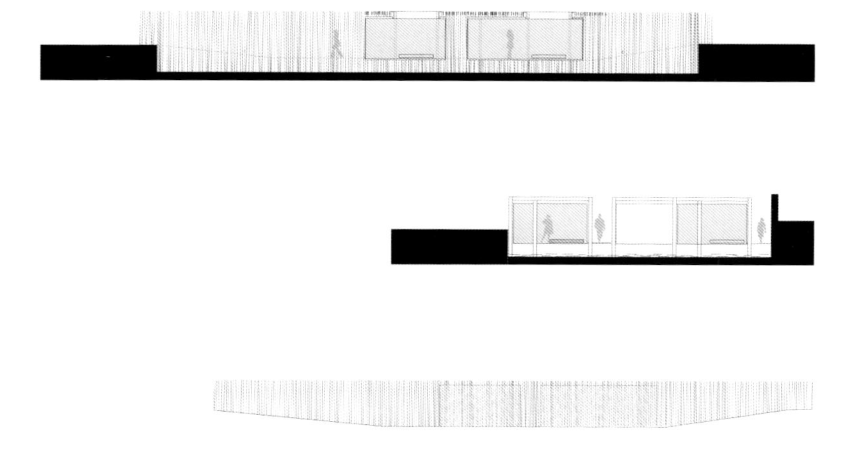

RCR ARANDA PIGEM VILALTA ARQUITECTES | OLOT

PUBLIC TOILETS IN THE FOREST

Olot, Spain | 1998

RCR ARANDA PIGEM VILALTA ARQUITECTES | OLOT
RIDAURA SOCIAL CENTER
Olot, Spain | 2000

ruun's
GALLERI

SCHMIDT HAMMER LASSEN ARCHITECTS | ÅRHUS
KPMG BUILDING
Århus, Denmark | 2004

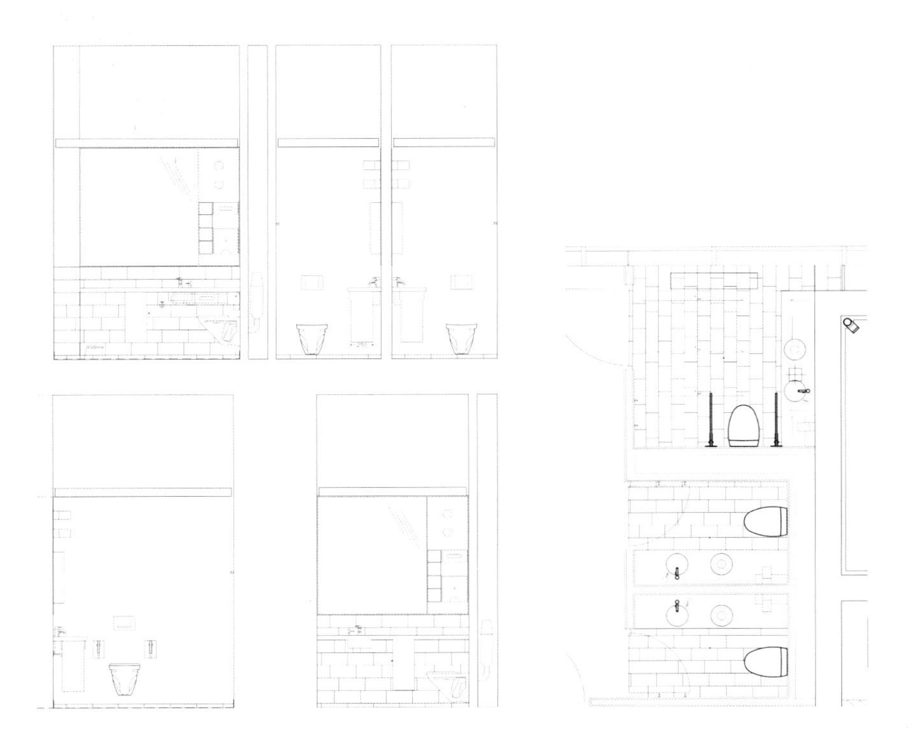

SHH ARCHITECTS & DESIGN CONSULTANTS | LONDON
ANGELS THE COSTUMIERS
London, United Kingdom | 2002

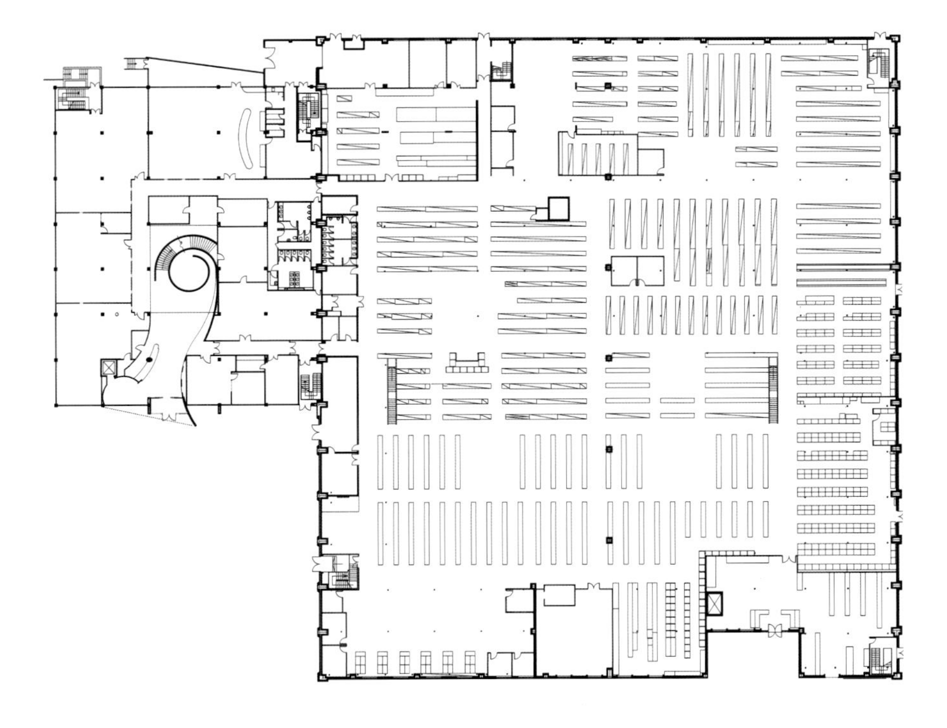

1A
2A

1A
1A

SHUHEI ENDO ARCHITECT INSTITUTE | OSAKA

HALFTECTURE OJ

Osaka, Japan | 2005

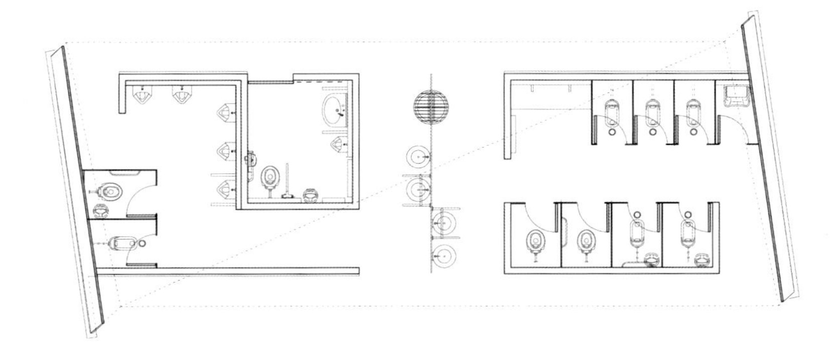

SHUHEI ENDO ARCHITECT INSTITUTE | OSAKA

HALFTECTURE OO

Osaka, Japan | 2005

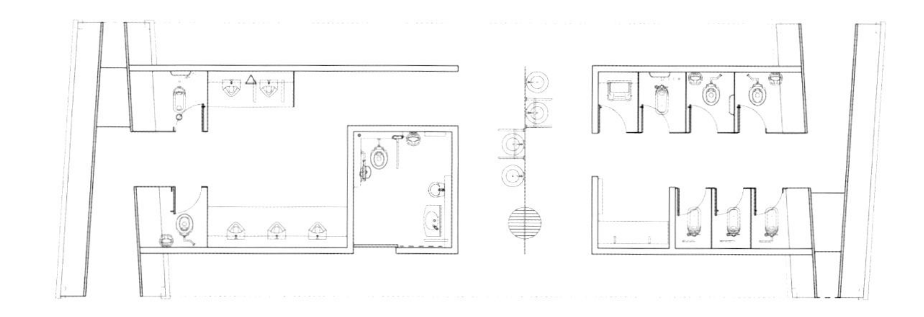

SQUARE ONE | BUCHAREST
EMBRYO
Bucharest, Romania | 2005

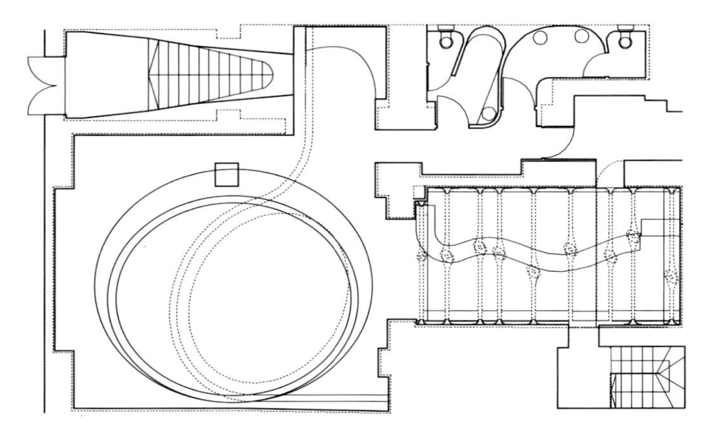

push

STUDIO 63 ARCHITECTURE & DESIGN | FLORENCE

SIXTY HOTEL

Riccione, Italy | 2006

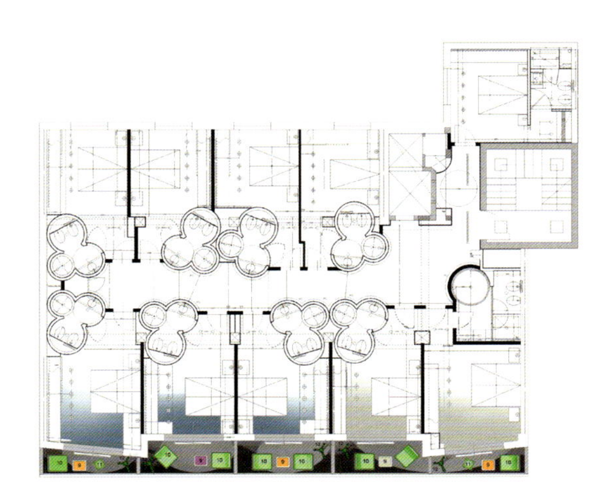

Jon burgerman 2006

STUDIO DI ARCHITETTURA MARCO CASTELLETTI | ERBA
BEACH FACILITIES ON THE SEGRINO RIVERBANK
Como, Italy | 2003

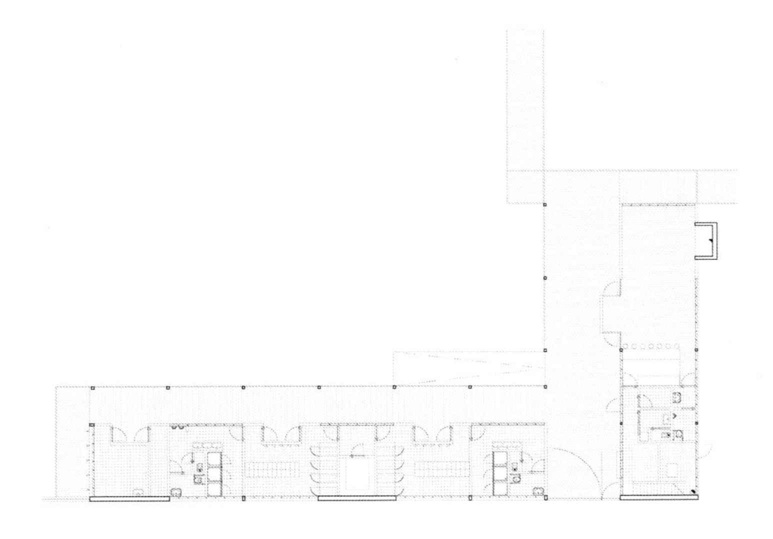

BAR

TERESA SAPEY ESTUDIO DE ARQUITECTURA | MADRID

ISOLÉE STORE

Madrid, Spain | 2006

TOOD SAUNDERS & TOMMIE WILHELMSEN | BERGEN
AURLAND LOOKOUT POINT
Aurland, Norway | 2005

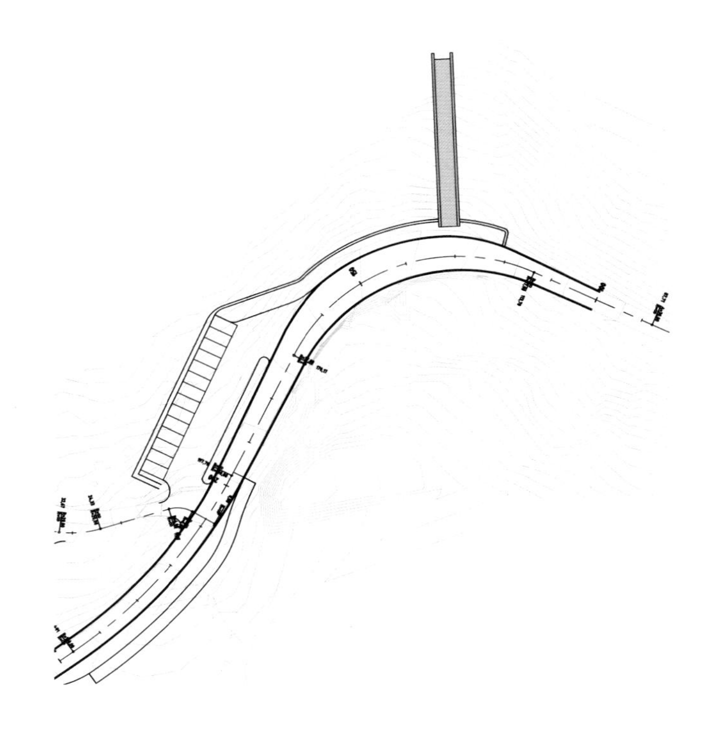

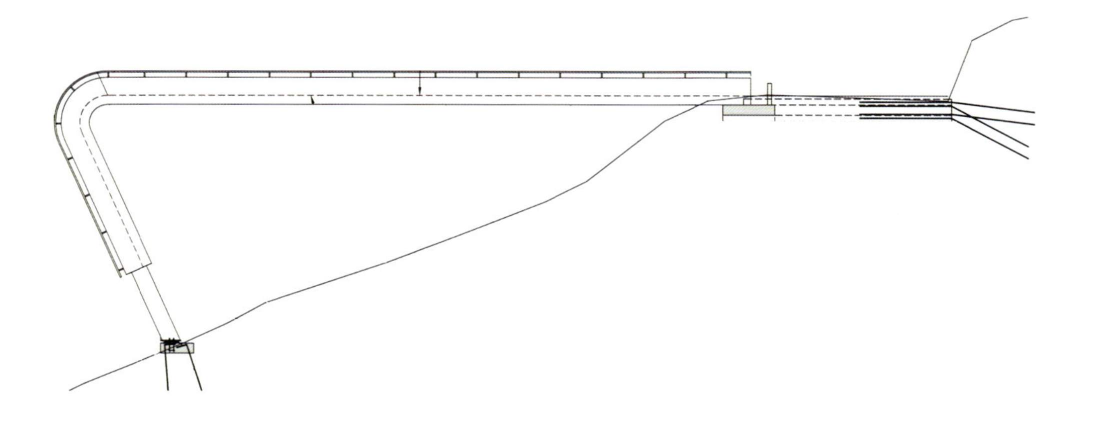

123DV Architectuur & Consult bv
St-jobsweg 30A
3024 EJ Rotterdam, The Netherlands
P +31 010 478 20 64
F +31 010 425 47 64
info@123dv.nl
www.123dv.nl
Restrooms in Jaarbeurs Utrecht
Photos © Christiaan de Bruijne

3Deluxe Transdisciplinary Design
Schwalbacher Strasse 74
D-65183 Wiesbaden, Germany
P +49 611 9522 0510
F +49 611 9522 0522
inexterior@3deluxe.de
www.3deluxe.de
Cocoon Club
Photos © Emanuel Raab

3RW Architects
PB 1131
5809 Bergen, Norway
P +47 55 36 55 36
F +47 55 36 55 37
3rw@3rw.no
www.3rw.no
Flydalsjuvet Viewpoint and Service Buildings
Photos © 3RW Architects
Hereiane Service Building
Photos © 3RW Architects

Acconci Studio
20 Jay Street, suite 215
Brooklyn, NY 11201, USA
P +1 718 852 6591
F +1 718 624 3178
www.acconci.com
Murinsel
Photos © Angelo Kaunat

Alonso Balaguer & Arquitectos Asociados
Bac de Roda 40
08019 Barcelona, Spain
P +34 93 303 41 60
F +34 93 303 41 61
estudi@alonsobalaguer.com
www.alonsobalaguer.com
Duet Sports
Photos © Alonso Balaguer & Arquitectos Asociados
02 Fitness Center
Photos © Josep M. Molinos

Amalgam
23 Old Street
EC1V 9HG London, United Kingdom
P +44 20 7250 4123
F +44 20 7250 4126
www.amalgam.co.uk
Bullring Shopping Center
Photos © Phillip Vile

Andrea Viviani
Via Eremitano 12
35138 Padova, Italy
P +39 049 661 461
F +39 049 875 676
a.viviani@awn.it
www.andreaviviani.it
Multiplex Cinecity Trieste
Photos © Alberto Ferrero

Anthony Kleinepier
Vestdijk 141A
5611CB Eindhoven, The Netherlands
P +31 40 213 25 45
F +31 40 213 25 45
www.anthonykleinepier.nl
De Effenaar
Photos © Michiel van Lierop, Paul Baudoin

Architecture Workshop Ltd
PO 9572, Wellington, New Zealand
P +64 4 473 4438
F +64 4 473 9572
email@archwksp.co.nz
www.archwksp.co.nz
Oriental Parade
Photos © Simon Devitt

Atelier van Lieshout
Keilestraat 43E
3029 BP Rotterdam, The Netherlands
P +31 10 244 09 71
F +31 10 244 09 72
www.ateliervanlieshout.com
Toilet Units Museum Boijmans van Beuningen
Photos © Atelier van Lieshout

Blobb/Analía Segal
387 14th Street 1
Brooklyn, NY 11215, USA
P +1 347 613 80 78
analiasegal@verizon.net
www.blobb.us
Blobb
Photos © Blobb

Bob Copray
Merovingersweg 4
5616JA Eindhoven, The Netherlands
P +31 65 375 60 30
www.bobcopray.nl
De Effenaar
Photos © Michiel van Lierop, Paul Baudoin

Buckley Gray Yeoman
Studio 5.04. The Tea Building
56 Shoreditch High Street
London E1 6JJ, United Kingdom
P +44 20 7033 9913
F +44 20 7033 9914
www.buckleygrayyeoman.com
Jo Shmo
Photos © Chris Gascoigne

Camenzind Evolution Ltd
Samariterstrasse 5
8032 Zurich, Switzerland
P +41 44 253 9500
F +41 44 253 9510
Zurich@camenzindevolution.com
www.camenzindevolution.com
Siemens Restaurants
Photos © Peter Würmli

Changduk Kim & Youngki Hong
JungAm Bldg 7F, 952-20 Bongcheon 1(il)-dong,
Gwanak-gu
151-051 Seoul, South Korea
www.universal-toilet.com
Universal Toilet
Photos © Changduk Kim & Youngki Hong

David Collins Studio
74 Farm Lane
London SW6 1QA, United Kingdom
P +44 20 7835 5000
F +44 20 7835 5100
studio@davidcollins.com
www.davidcollins.com
Kabarets Prophecy
Photos © Adrian Wilson

Designrichtung gmbh
Luisenstrasse 25
CH-8005 Zurich, Switzerland
P +41 44 422 53 20
F +41 44 422 53 27
info@designrichtung.ch
www.designrichtung.ch
Geberit Headquarters
Photos © Tom Bisig
Geberit Training Center
Photos © Tom Bisig

Dizel & Sate Ab
Östgötagatan 16
116 25 Stockholm, Sweden
P +46 8 545 141 48
contact@dizelsate.com
www.dizelsate.com
Astoria
Photos © Mandus Rudholm

Elia Felices
Lepanto 309-311, L-B
08025 Barcelona, Spain
P/F +34 93 435 49 71
info@eliafelices.com
www.eliafelices.com
Dalai Discotheque
Photos © Rafael Vargas

García & Ruiz Architecture Design
Antonio Acuña 14, 2 B
28009 Madrid, Spain
P +34 915 774 518
F +34 914 311 999
e.mail.ggrv@nauta.es
www.ggrvarquitectos.com
Cepsa Restrooms
Photos © Pedro Mahamud

Germán del Sol
Camino Las Flores 11441
Las Condes, Santiago de Chile, Chile
www.germandelsol.cl
Baths in Atacama
Photos © Guy Wemborne

Gregory Burgess Pty Ltd Architects
10 York Street
Richmond, Victoria 3121, Australia
P +61 3 9411 0600
F +61 3 9411 0699
gba@gregoryburgessarchitects.com.au
www.gregoryburgessarchitects.com.au
Highway Rest Areas
Photos © Photohub/Ben Wrigley

Hassan Abdullah
1 Club Row
London E1 6JX, United Kingdom
P +44 20 7613 1924
info@lestroisgarcons.com
www.lestroisgarcons.com
Les Trois Garçons
Photos © Yael Pincus

HSH Architects
Grafická 20
20150 00 Prague, Czech Republic
P +420 233 354 417
www.hsharchitekti.cz
Archdiocesan Museum in Olomouc
Photos © Ester Havlová

Jestico & Whiles
1 Cobourg Street
London NW1 2HP, United Kingdom
P +44 20 7380 0382
F +44 20 7380 0511
www.jesticowhiles.com
Princess Diana of Wales Memorial Playground
Photos © James Morris
Village Cinemas Multiplex
Photos © Ales Jungmann

Johannes Torpe
Skoubogade 1, 1/DK-1158
Copenhagen, Denmark
P +45 7025 5556
info@johannestorpe.com
www.johannestorpe.com
Nasa
Photos © Jens Stoltze

Kadawittfeldarchitektur
Aureliusstraße 2
52064 Aachen, Austria
P +49 241 946 90 0
F +49 241 946 90 20
office@kadawittfeldarchitektur.de
www.kadawittfeldarchitektur.de
Zeughaus
Photos © Angelo Kaunat

Kraske Architecture & Yacht Design
Türkenstr. 21 RGB
80799 Munich, Germany
P +49 89 28788689
F +49 89 28788687
info@jochenkraske.de
www.jochenkraske.de
Tantris
Photos © Kraske Architecture and Yacht Design

Lacock Gullam
Oblique Studios
Stamford Works, Gillett Street
London N16 8JH, United Kingdom
P +44 20 7503 4001
studio@lacockgullam.co.uk
www.lacockgullam.co.uk
Butterfly On-Street Urinal
Photos © Speller Milner Design

Marcelo Sodré
Rua Salvador Correia 628
18030-130 Sorocaba
São Paulo, Brazil
sodre@splicenet.com.br
www.marcelosodre.com.br
Casacor
Photos © Tuca Reinés

Matali Crasset Productions
26 Rue du Buisson Saint Louis
75010 Paris, France
P +33 1 42 40 99 89
F +33 1 42 40 99 98
www.matalicrasset.com
Hi Hotel
Photos © Geoffrey Cottenceau, Patrick Gries

Miró Rivera Architects
505 Powell Street
Austin, TX 78703, USA
P + 1 512 477 7016
F + 1 512 476 7672
michael@mirorivera.com
www.mirorivera.com
Lady Bird Lake Hike and Bike Trail Restroom
Photos © Paul Finkel

Monica Bonvicini
c/o Galleria Emi Fontana
Viale Bligny 42
20136 Milan, Italy
P +39 025 832 2237
F +39 025 830 6855
emi@micronet.it
Don't Miss a Sec
Photos © c/o Galleria Emi Fontana

MVRDV
Dunantstraat 10
3024 BC Rotterdam, The Netherlands
P +31 10 477 28 60
F +31 10 477 36 27
www.mvrdv.nl
Lloyd Hotel
Photos © Allard van der Hoek

Pentagram
204 Fifth Avenue
New York, NY 10010, USA
P + 1 212 683 7000
F + 1 212 532 0181
www.pentagram.com
Locker Rooms and Bathrooms in Arizona Cardinals Stadium
Photos © Pentagram

Pierluigi Piu
Via E. Besta 6
09129 Cagliari, Italy
P +39 340 529 3381
pierlugipiu@virgilio.it
Olivomare Restaurant
Photos © Giorgio Dettori, Pierluigi Piu

Plastik Architects Ltd
Panther House
38 Mount Pleasant
London WC1X 0AN, United Kingdom
P +44 20 7713 0728
F +44 20 7713 6594
www.plastik-architects.net
Gravesend Public Toilets
Photos © Robin Hayes

Playground Melbourne/Fady Hachem
Level 2, 2 Drewery Place
3000 Melbourne, Australia
P +61 1 3007 34560
F +61 1 3007 23451
fh@playgroundmelbourne.com
www.playgroundmelbourne.com
Valve
Photos © Shania Shegedyn

Purpur. Architektur
Getreidemarkt 14
1010 Vienna, Austria
P +43 1 9203492
F +43 1 9203492 34
studio@purpur.cc
www.purpur.cc
Murinsel
Photos © Angelo Kaunat

RCR Aranda Pigem Vilalta Arquitectes
Passeig de Blay 34, 2
17800 Olot, Spain
P +34 972 269 105
F +34 972 267 558
www.rcrarquitectes.es
Pavilions in Les Cols Restaurant
Photos © Eugeni Pons
Public Toilets in the Forest
Photos © Jordi Miralles
Ridaura Social Center
Photos © Jordi Miralles

Schmidt Hammer Lassen Architects
Clemensborg, Aaboulevarden 37
5117 DK-8000 Århus, Denmark
P +45 86 20 1900
F +45 86 18 4513
www.shl.dk
KPMG Building
Photos © Adam Mørk

SHH Architects & Design Consultants
1 Vencourt Place, Ravenscourt Park
Hammersmith, London W6 9NU
United Kingdom
P +44 20 8600 4171
F +44 20 8600 4181
www.shh.co.uk
Angels the Costumiers
Photos © Francesca Yorke

Shuhei Endo Architect Institute
6F,3-21,Suehiro-cho, Kita-ku
Osaka 530-0053, Japan
P +81 (6)6312 7455
F +81 (6)6312 7456
www.paramodern.com
Halftecture OJ
Photos © Yoshiharu Matsumura
Halftecture OO
Photos © Yoshiharu Matsumura

Smedsvig Landskapsarkitekter
Øvre Korskirkesmauet 2B
5018 Bergen, Norway
P +47 55 21 04 70
F +47 55 21 04 80
www.smedsvig-landskap.no
Flydalsjuvet Viewpoint and Service Buildings
Photos © 3RW Architects

Square One
C. A. Rosetti 42, ap. 4, sector 2
Bucharest, Romania
P +40 031 405 53 79
F +40 031 405 53 80
office@squareone.ro
www.squareone.ro
Embryo
Photos © Nicu Ilfoveanu

Studio 63 Architecture & Design
Via Santo Spirito 6
50125 Florence, Italy
P +39 055 239 9252
F +39 055 265 8419
info@studio63.it
www.studio63.it
Sixty Hotel
Photos © Yael Pincus

Studio di Architettura Marco Castelletti
Erba (Co) via Battisti 7/L
Eupilio, Como, Italy
P +39 031 645 600
F +39 031 646 633
studio@marcocastelletti.it
www.marcocastelletti.it
Beach Facilities on the Segrino Riverbank
Photos © Filippo Simonetti

Teresa Sapey Estudio de Arquitectura
Francisco Campos 13
28002 Madrid, Spain
P +34 917 450 876
F +34 915 644 300
estudio4@teresasapey.com
www.teresasapey.com
Isolée Store
Photos © Jordi Miralles

Tood Saunders & Tommie Wilhelmsen
Vestre torggate 22
NO-5015 Bergen, Norway
P +47 55 36 85 06
F +47 97 52 57 61
www.saunders.no
Aurland Lookout Point
Photos © Todd Saunders

published and distributed worldwide by
daab gmbh
friesenstr. 50
d-50670 köln

p +49 - 221 - 913 927 0
f +49 - 221 - 913 927 20

mail@daab-online.com
www.daab-online.com

publisher ralf daab

creative director feyyaz

editorial project by loft publications

editor and texts marta serrats
layout guillermo pfaff puigmartí
english translation equipo de edición
german translation equipo de edición
french translation equipo de edición
italian translation equipo de edición

printed in italy
www.zanardi.it

isbn 978-3-86654-023-1